Bridging Cultures in Early Care and Education

A Training Module

Bridging Cultures in Early Care and Education

A Training Module

Marlene Zepeda
Janet Gonzalez-Mena
Carrie Rothstein-Fisch
Elise Trumbull

Routledge
Taylor & Francis Group
New York London

About WestEd

WestEd, a nonprofit research, development, and service agency, works with education and other communities to promote excellence, achieve equity, and improve learning for children, youth, and adults. Although WestEd serves Arizona, California, Nevada, and Utah as one of the nation's Regional Educational Laboratories, the agency's work extends throughout the United States and abroad. It has 16 offices nationwide, from Washington and Boston to Arizona and Southern California, and its headquarters in San Francisco. For more information about WestEd, visit WestEd.org; call (415) 565-3000 or, toll-free, (877) 4-WestEd, or write: WestEd, 730 Harrison Street, San Francisco, CA 94107-1242.

The development of *Bridging Cultures in Early Care and Education* was funded in part with funds from the Institute of Education Sciences, U.S. Department of Education, under contract #ED-01-CO-0012. Its contents do not necessarily reflect the views or policies of the Department of Education.

First published by Lawrence Erlbaum Associates, Inc., Publishers
10 Industrial Avenue
Mahwah, New Jersey 07430

Transferred to digital printing 2010 by Routledge

Routledge

270 Madison Avenue
New York, NY 10016

2 Park Square, Milton Park
Abingdon, Oxon OX14 4RN, UK

Cover design by Kathryn Houghtaling Lacey

WestEd

Library of Congress Cataloging-in-Publication Data

Bridging cultures in early care and education : a training module / Marlene Zepeda . . . [et al.].
p. cm.
Includes bibliographical references and index.
ISBN 0-8058-5641-2 (pbk. : alk. paper)
1. Early childhood education—Social aspects—United States. 2. Educational anthropology—United States.
I. Zepeda, Marlene, 1950–

LB1139.25.B745 2005
372.21—dc22 2005051371
CIP

10 9 8 7 6 5 4 3 2 1

Contents

Preface

About This Book

Bridging Cultures in Early Care and Education: A Training Module is a resource designed to help preservice and in-service early childhood educators, including infant/toddler caregivers, understand the role of culture in their programs. It can also be used by professionals who work with children and their families in a variety of other roles, such as social workers, special educators, and early interventionists.

Why should early childhood professionals consider the role of culture? Increasingly, home- and center-based staff and providers work with children and families who come from cultural backgrounds different from their own. Early care and education programs are generally the first settings where children may be away from their families for extended periods. Furthermore, the early years are the time when identity formation begins. Thus, if children are to identify closely with their family and culture, their experience with child-care providers must be culturally consistent with that at home. This is especially true during children's first 3 years of life (Lally, 1995). When a young child's family and his or her outside caregiver come from different cultural backgrounds and operate with different cultural expectations, there is greater potential for the child to experience difficulty with identity formation. Also, in such circumstances, adjustment between the home and the child-care setting can be more difficult for all involved (Bowman & Stott, 1994).

Most families with children have more contact with early childhood professionals than they do with educators once their children enter elementary school and start moving up the grades. This first contact is especially important because it helps form families' attitudes toward school, educators, and other child-serving professionals. Thus, the early childhood years provide caregivers and early educators an opportunity to make a positive impact not only on children's adjustment to outside care and education but also on long-term relationships between families and professionals. Simply stated, early childhood is a critical time to begin establishing common ground between teachers (including infant/toddler caregivers, and other professionals) and the children and families they serve.

In fact, understanding, respecting, and valuing diversity should be a two-way process between early childhood professionals and those they serve. When strong family–professional partnerships exist, practices at home and within the program can be mutually supportive. Certainly, engagement between home and school contributes to children's educational success throughout their school experience (Henderson & Mapp, 2002), and teachers' cultural knowledge can support greater parent involvement (Trumbull, Greenfield, Rothstein-Fisch, & Quiroz, 2001).

An Organizing Framework for Understanding Culture

This book is an outgrowth of our interest in exploring how early childhood educators can use the organizing concepts of *individualism* and *collectivism* as a means of understanding cultural differences between themselves and the families they serve. These concepts, explained and illustrated in the following chapters, have been shown to be highly useful in improving home–school understanding across cultures. The two-part framework of individualism and collectivism is the foundation of our previous work with elementary school teachers and the students and families they serve. The framework has been said to be "nonthreatening" because it describes the value systems of cultures in a nonjudgmental way (Trumbull, Diaz-Meza, Hasan, & Rothstein-Fisch, 2001). This makes it a safe way to learn about cultures—one's own as well as those of others.

Certainly, a single training session could never fully prepare anyone to deal with all cultural issues in early childhood settings. The Bridging Cultures in Early Care and Education (BC–ECE) module is just a beginning step in the understanding of cultural differences and the development of the cultural competency needed for working with young children and their families.

Audiences for the Training Module

The BC–ECE module is designed for both preservice and in-service training. The material can also be used in college courses focused on early childhood education and child development. The module will be of interest to Head Start and Early Head Start programs, state preschool programs, private/nonprofit early care or education programs, family child-care providers, home visitors, early interventionists, special educators, and family service staff. For facilitators who use the WestEd Program for Infant-Toddler Caregivers (PITC) training model, the BC–ECE module is a natural follow-up to the cultural sessions in *Module IV: Culture, Family, and Providers*. It is also a complementary follow-up to training that deals with special needs populations, such as Beginning Together, the California Institute on Human Services' training for full inclusion. The module can be presented in 2 hours or expanded to as much as a full day, with additional follow-up. It can also be incorporated into ongoing staff meetings on a regular basis. Thus, it is flexible enough to meet the needs of a range of users.

Organization of the Training Module

The organization of the BC–ECE module is intended to make it as easy as possible for educators and others involved with professional development to understand the individualism–collectivism framework in the context of early childhood care and education and to facilitate that understanding in those they work with. It is our hope that professional development specialists will be able to use the activities and examples in the module to develop effective presentations that engage and inspire. Chapter 1 introduces the BC–ECE approach and provides a brief history and explanation of the training module. Chapter 1 also presents the conceptual framework of individualism and collectivism, which is at the heart of the training.

Chapter 2 provides the information needed for a 2-hour workshop, including a script and notes to the facilitator. Because of the complexity of the concepts introduced in the module, the training should *minimally* be 2 hours in length.

The script is not intended to be read word for word. Rather, it is offered as a guide, based on an approach that has been pilot tested several times. The training was conceived to be delivered in a guided lecture–discussion format, with activities interspersed throughout the 2 hours. The activities are designed to prompt dialogue and participant interaction in small groups. To assist facilitators, key concepts are noted at the beginning of each section in the script.

The facilitator notes are added to support the optimal use of the module and include tips drawn from the experience of the authors, as well as cues for using the overhead transparencies and handouts, directions for the activities, and ideas about places to stop for discussion. Because we encourage facilitators to make this training their own, there is space in the margins to write notes related to personal experience or to mark examples that might be particularly relevant to different audiences.

Appendix A contains transparency masters for the overheads referenced in the script in chapter 2, and Appendix B contains masters for suggested handouts. We have intentionally placed these materials in separate appendices to make duplication easier. It should be noted that some overheads and handouts are the same. This replication was intended to provide flexibility for the facilitator: Overheads can be used in whole-group discussion and handouts can be used for small-group work. This allows the facilitator to gear the presentation to participants' needs and preferences.

Recognizing that a 2-hour workshop can be but a small first step toward developing the deeper cultural understanding needed by early childhood professionals, chapter 3 provides ideas for augmenting the training and expanding it over a longer period. It proposes additional activities, some of them targeted to particular audiences, such as staff working in early care and education settings, special educators, early interventionists, and family service staff. In addition, the suggested strategies can be used with students in early childhood education classes. Chapter 3 also recommends resources that can complement Bridging Cultures training by linking it to other diversity material.

Finally, the appendices present (a) information about a study highlighted in the presentation that quantifies the degree of individualism in various countries, (b) recommendations for the best ways to use the module, (c) data from training workshops where the BC–ECE module was pilot tested, and (d) an annotated bibliography describing key ideas and concepts underlying BC–ECE training.

About the Authors

Marlene Zepeda is a professor of Child and Family Studies at California State University, Los Angeles. She has studied the development of Spanish-speaking children and their families residing in southern California.

Janet Gonzalez-Mena is an internationally recognized leader in multicultural early childhood teacher education and has published widely on this topic. Her book, *Multicultural Issues in Child Care*, is in its fourth edition and has been retitled *Diversity in Early Care and Education: Honoring Differences.*

Carrie Rothstein-Fisch was on the original Bridging Cultures team and is co-coordinator of the Masters Program in Early Childhood Education at the Michael D. Eisner School of Education at California State University, Northridge. She developed the *Bridging Cultures Teacher Education Module* and edited the *Readings for the Bridging Cultures Education Module* targeted for elementary school teachers.

Elise Trumbull is an independent consultant and was the director of the Bridging Cultures Project at WestEd from 1996 to 2003. She has directed the module development project and is the coauthor of numerous books and articles about culture and language in education, including *Bridging Cultures Between Home and School: A Guide for Teachers.*

Acknowledgments

Our first thank you must go to the A. L. Mailman Family Foundation, which supported the development of this training module. Readers who are interested in the other projects supported by the foundation can find this information online at http://www.mailman.org. We are also indebted to the Foundation for Child Development (http://www.ffcd.org) for providing seed money to seek funding for the Bridging Cultures in Early Care and Education Project.

We appreciate the support of WestEd, a nonprofit research, development, and service organization that focuses on education and human development and that houses the Regional Educational Laboratory serving Arizona, California, Nevada, and Utah. Through a federal grant from the Department of Education, WestEd supported the initial Bridging Cultures research and development. It has also supported the development of this module and continues to make Bridging Cultures materials available through its catalogues and Web site (http://www.WestEd.org). We are particularly indebted to Joy Zimmerman, whose careful editing has strengthened the final version of the module. (Additional information about Bridging Cultures can be found at http://www.WestEd.org/bridging cultures.)

Although she is not an author of this module, Patricia Greenfield, professor of Psychology at University of California, Los Angeles, is a partner in the work and has given much support to the authors during its development. It was her research with Blanca Quiroz and Catherine Raeff that formed the foundation of the Bridging Cultures Project in 1996. The seven original Bridging Cultures Project teachers must also be recognized as a force behind the scenes: Marie Altchech, Catherine Daley, Katherine Eyler, Elvia Hernandez, Giancarlo Mercado, Amada Pérez, and Pearl Saitzyk. They made the framework come alive with their school-based innovations and advocacy for children and families.

We have also been fortunate to have the input of the Bridging Cultures Advisory Committee: Jamie Almanzán, Michael Ballard-Rosa, Rosita Fabian, Rodney Gillead, Joel Gordon, Stephanie Graham, Eugene Kerr, Sharon Seidman Milburn,

Kari Knutson Miller, Lupita Tannatt, Roland Tharp, Jo Topps, Tony Vang, Elisa Velasquez-Andrade, Liz Wolfe, and Marlene Zepeda. Much of the final impetus for creation of the module came from these California educators, several of whom are early childhood specialists. And, as can be seen, one of the committee members (Marlene Zepeda) became an author of this module.

We are grateful to the Los Angeles County Office of Education, which allowed us to pilot the module with 70 of its affiliated educators and care providers. The pilot participants generously offered us their insights, based on wide-ranging experience—all of which helped us select the appropriate content and format for the module. We also received extremely helpful feedback from the more than 100 participants attending our session at the annual National Association for the Education of Young Children Professional Development Conference in Portland, Oregon (June 2003). And special thanks are due to the students enrolled in Issues and Theories in Early Childhood Education (EPC 632) at California State University, Northridge, who helped Carrie Rothstein-Fisch pilot test an earlier version of the module.

Special thanks to Bill Edwards of Magna Systems, Bryan Fisch, Miriam Godinez, Carrie Rothstein-Fisch, Leslie Weinstock, and Marlene Zepeda for the photographs throughout this book. We gratefully acknowledge the families and staff of the California State University, Northridge, Child and Family Studies Center and the Anna Bing Arnold Child Development Center at California State University, Los Angeles. In particular, our thanks are extended to Christa C. Dunlap and Patricia Ramirez-Ulloa, Assistant Directors at each of these child development centers.

Finally, we thank those who have provided valuable and critical reviews of earlier versions of the module: Isaura Barrera, Judy Cashell, Yolanda Garcia, Joel Gordon, Christina Lopez Morgan, Virginia Reynolds, and Sheila Signer. These educators and service providers are engaged in important work that is inevitably more than full-time; therefore, their willingness to give the module a thorough read is all the more appreciated.

Chapter 1

Introduction to the Training Module

Before they come to school, all children learn and develop in their own unique and highly diverse linguistic, social, and cultural context. When previous learning and development are nurtured in early education programs, the overall benefits of early education are enhanced.

—National Association for the Education of Young Children licensure standards (Hyson, 2003, p. 38)

Like their colleagues working in elementary and secondary schools, early childhood professionals in the United States serve a highly diverse population. Some of this diversity results from the steady influx of immigrant families from a variety of cultural backgrounds. But there is also cultural diversity among children whose parents are second-generation immigrants and even among those whose families have lived in the United States for many generations. The diversity of the population is increasing and is expected to do so for some time (see *Growing Diversity*, p. 2). This growing diversity has moved the National Association for the Education of Young Children (NAEYC) to require early childhood programs seeking accreditation to demonstrate that they "use linguistic and cultural diversity as resources rather than seeing diversity as a deficit or problem" (Hyson, 2003, p. 38). Similarly, Head Start has developed "multicultural principles" that focus on the importance of culture, identity, and support for the primary language (www.bmcc.org/Headstart/Cultural/).

Many early childhood professionals recognize the value of learning about the cultures of the children with whom they work but are not sure how to approach the task. Others don't recognize diversity because the youngsters in their class or center don't *look* different from one another. They may not realize that children who appear to have the same ethnicity can, nonetheless, be tremendously diverse in terms of their home values. Although early childhood professionals may make efforts to learn about the cultural backgrounds of the children they serve, they may find the effort overwhelming when the children represent several countries or even multiple regions and cultures within the same country.

For example, one kindergarten teacher decided that to better understand her students, she should start studying Mexican culture. "Then," she said, "I realized that the children in my class came from many distinct regions, each with different histories and traditions. I just knew that I would never know enough. I had to give up trying" (Rothstein-Fisch, Greenfield, & Trumbull, 1999, p. 64).

What is culture exactly and how are we using the term in the present training module? Culture has many different definitions, but a simple one that can be applied to the Bridging Cultures in Early Care and Education (BC–ECE) module is "a set of values, beliefs and ways of thinking about the world that influences everyday behavior" (Trumbull & Farr, 2005). Culture is transmitted from one generation to the next in multiple ways, both explicitly, in conversations and direct guidance, and implicitly, in daily practices such as childrearing. It is when disparities in the values and belief systems of different individuals become evident that culture comes into focus.

Bridging Cultures in Early Care and Education: A Training Module was conceived to address the frustration of those who believe they will "never know enough" and to open the eyes of those who may not yet recognize the need to understand cultural differences. BC–ECE training helps teachers and providers become "cultural bridges" between children and families and early care and education settings. The framework underlying this module has proved useful for educators because of its accessibility. There are only two basic concepts to remember—*individualism* and *collectivism.* These concepts are used to illustrate how cultural beliefs and values shape attitudes and behaviors.

This module was inspired by previous research (Greenfield, Quiroz, & Raeff, 2000; Raeff, Greenfield, & Quiroz, 2000) showing that deep, but invisible, cultural values influence how teachers, students, and parents or guardians approach home- and school-based problems. Moreover, the research shows that when elementary grade teachers learn about the priorities and value orientations of their students' families, one result is greatly improved relationships with those families (Trumbull, Diaz-Meza, Hasan, & Rothstein-Fisch, 2001; Trumbull, Greenfield, Rothstein-Fisch, & Quiroz, 2001).

We believe that participation in BC–ECE training will yield similar benefits for early childhood educators and caregivers—helping them better understand the home cultures of children and families. Understanding cultural differences is especially important for those dealing with young children be-

Growing Diversity

According to Child Trends (http://www.childtrends.org), a national children's research organization, the percentage of children from racial and ethnic minority groups is projected to increase for the next 20 years. By 2020, approximately 46% of all children ages 0 to 5 will come from racial and ethnic minority backgrounds. Projections for 2020 are that the child population will be 1% American Indian/Native Alaskan, 6% Asian/Pacific Islander, 14% African American, 25% Latino, and 55% White. With this diversity, the issue of multiracial and/or multiethnic identities will become increasingly important. In the 2000 Census, mixed-race individuals accounted for 2.4% of the national population, and this group is projected to increase. Also, the number of individuals born outside of the United States continues to grow and with this rise is an increase in the number of people who speak a home language other than English (see U.S. Census Bureau Reports, from McKinnon, 2003; Ogunwole, 2003; Ramirez & de la Cruz, 2003; Reeves & Bennett, 2003).

cause it is during children's preschool years that families have their first experiences with the out-of-home child care and education systems, experiences that can set the tone for future school–home interactions. At this early stage of children's lives, solid rapport between professionals and families is also important because of the growing emphasis on ensuring children's "school readiness," defined increasingly in academic terms (Shonkoff & Phillips, 2000). This means that expectations for children from "nonmainstream" cultural backgrounds to conform to "mainstream" norms may be greater than in the past—or, at least appearing earlier in children's lives. In the face of such pressures, cross-cultural understanding is all the more important.

The Bridging Cultures Project

The Bridging Cultures Project began in 1996 as a professional development effort to improve cross-cultural understanding in elementary school settings. The project is based on research studies that point to the importance of understanding cultural value differences between the home and the school in order to avoid or resolve problems that affect teachers, parents, and children (Greenfield et al., 2000; Raeff et al., 2000). A project evaluation revealed that the elementary school teachers (four Latino and three European American) who participated in Bridging Cultures' first professional development acquired a deeper understanding and appreciation of their students' cultures (as well as their own), improved their instruction and classroom management, and experienced better relationships with the families of their students (Trumbull, Diaz-Meza, et al., 2001). Although the project has focused on immigrant Latino families and children, the framework it uses has been applied to many other cultures (Hofstede, 2001, Appendix C).

The kinds of change experienced by participating teachers are illustrated by one teacher's comment that after Bridging Cultures training, she felt "less isolated and more heartened. I'm more aware of my individualistic tendencies. I have made an effort to connect more with parents. Awareness of this model and the possibility of change is encouraging" (Trumbull, Greenfield, Rothstein-Fisch, & Maynard, 2005, p. 25). The Bridging Cultures Project has yielded a number of publications describing its approach to culture and presenting research findings validating the usefulness of the individualism and collectivism framework.[1]

Need for Bridging Cultures in Early Childhood

The need for a version of Bridging Cultures for early childhood professionals became apparent when one of the authors, Carrie Rothstein-Fisch, made several presentations to teachers and staff involved with Head Start. Evaluations from those trainings were very favorable with regard to the usefulness of the framework, but workshop participants asked for more examples, hands-on activities, and visual aids relevant to early childhood. Inspired by that feedback and by encouragement from the Bridging Cultures Advisory Committee, we have taken the basic framework of individualism and collectivism explained in earlier Bridging Cultures publications and applied it to early childhood settings using real-life examples and interactive activities.

[1]See www.WestEd.org/bridgingcultures.

It is our hope that the BC–ECE module can help meet the needs of early childhood professionals and others by giving them a way to think about the diverse and sometimes conflicting cultural priorities they see playing out in their settings. The training is intended to assist professionals in understanding their own actions and attitudes, as well as those of children, families, and colleagues with whom they work. Early childhood professionals are encouraged to review current practices in their own programs or other professional settings and to consider the underlying cultural values that are reflected in them. In doing so, they can consciously explore ways to better accommodate and support children and families from a range of cultural backgrounds.

The Framework: Individualism Versus Collectivism

Bridging Cultures in Early Care and Education introduces workshop participants to two contrasting value orientations: individualism and collectivism. Each orientation is associated with a different set of cultural priorities that, among other things, guide how members of a culture rear and educate their children. Focusing on this distinction is not the only way to think about cultural differences, but it has proven to be extremely useful for understanding many instances of cross-cultural misunderstanding.

Individualism

Individualism stresses independence and individual achievement, focusing on the needs of the individual, self-expression, and personal choice. It emphasizes the object world, particularly with respect to the concept of private property and the idea that objects are a source of learning about the physical world. When a preschool, infant program, or family child-care home operates primarily from an individualistic perspective, children are treated as unique and special individuals who need the opportunity to explore objects in their surroundings and to learn to become independent. The physical environment is also likely to reflect this perspective, with children having their own cubbies, lockers, or coat hooks identified as "theirs" and their names and pictures prominently displayed. It is also likely that parents are asked to put name tags on their child's clothing. Children are encouraged to take care of their property, take care of themselves (e.g., toileting, feeding, dressing), and use "their words" to identify their needs. All of these examples are signs that individualism is valued.

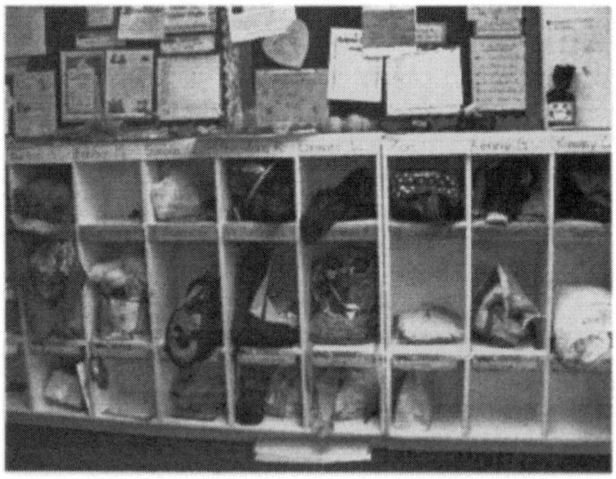

Photographer: Carrie Rothstein-Fisch

Collectivism

Although the United States as a whole values and encourages individuals' independence, most of the world tends to focus on the *inter*dependence of groups and individuals, reflecting the cultural value of collectivism. According to cross-cultural experts, a collectivistic value orientation is found in 70% of the world's cultures (Triandis, 1989).

Collectivism emphasizes social responsibility and the priority of group needs over individual needs. It stresses respect for authority and obligation to group norms. In collectivistic cultures, possessions are often shared, with objects being important in the context of human relationships, not in and of themselves. For instance, a toy or household object may be used as a source of interaction between a mother and child, but the child is not likely to be directed to play with it or investigate it independently. In this example, the object is viewed as a tool for emphasizing the relationship between the mother and the child, one based on interdependence, helping, and sharing. In collectivistic cultures there is also a strong emphasis on the family as a unit, not on each member per se.

Photographer: Miriam Godinez

When a preschool, infant program, or family child-care home emphasizes sharing and downplays the individual and his or her personal accomplishments in favor of the achievements of the group, it is exhibiting collectivistic values. Collectivistic practices that can be seen in early care and education settings include potluck meals as a means of sharing across many families, favoring large-group size for activities over small-group or individual interaction, and mixed-aged grouping where older children help and assist younger children.

We *Can* Build Cultural Bridges

Is it possible to reconcile the differences between collectivism and individualism? Can early childhood educators create links between those who are clearly collectivistic and those who are not? Can collectivistic families and children be made to feel at home in an individualistic environment, and vice versa?

Our project is predicated on the belief that the answer to all of these questions is *yes*. In fact, many early childhood care and education settings already reflect a good balance between collectivism and individualism. But they are more rare than they should be. This module is designed to help participants develop an appreciation for the contrasting patterns of care and education reflected in individualistic and collectivistic value orientations, to understand that they need not be mutually exclusive, and to explore how best to bridge and blend these two perspectives in early childhood and related settings.

Successful relationships between families and early childhood professionals—who themselves come from a variety of cultural backgrounds—can help pave the way to lifelong learning, not just about *how* cultural differences play out but about *why*. The underlying motivations—the why—for culture-based behaviors may be more easily sorted out and understood with the use of a framework (such as the individualism/collectivism framework) that helps organize our thoughts about ourselves and our observations of others.

The framework is explained in greater detail in chapter 2, along with charts outlining some of the most important features of individualism and collectivism.

Our Goals and Philosophy

Our goal in developing this training module is to help early childhood professionals and others who work with young children and their families recognize and address deep and abiding issues of power and equity. The power of a family is undermined when parents do not have a say in their children's care and education, and equity is jeopardized when services meet the needs of some children more than others. Families should be full partners in their children's care and education, and it is the primary responsibility of early education professionals and service providers to initiate these partnerships. Indeed, it is their professional obligation according to standards of the NAEYC and of Head Start.

Demonstrating understanding and respect for families' childrearing practices empowers families and contributes to educational equity for their children. Finding common ground between families and professionals is definitely in the best interest of children (Goldenberg, Gallimore, Reese, & Garnier, 2001; Gonzalez-Mena, 2001; Trumbull, Rothstein-Fisch, & Hernandez, 2003).

When it comes to their cultural values, families are neither superior nor inferior to each other; they are just different. Until families are accepted for who they are and what they value, early care and education programs will perpetuate inequities and may unintentionally facilitate the disappearance of vital cultural knowledge that resides within families. Consider the cost if families are not valued, a situation Amada Pérez, one of the original Bridging Cultures teachers, describes when speaking about her own experience growing up:

> We came to feel that the rules at school were more important than the rules at home. The school and the teacher were right. As a child, you begin to feel the conflict. Many of my brothers stopped communicating with the family and with my father because he was ignorant. (Rothstein-Fisch, 2003a, p. 89)

When two cultures meet, both are changed. But all too often members of "minority" cultures find themselves having to conform to the values and norms of the "mainstream" culture, potentially undermining the strength of the family. We believe that children and their families should not have to relinquish their cultural identity to benefit from early care and education.

Recognizing new sets of cultural values does not necessarily mean rejecting one's own values. We are not asking that early childhood professionals turn their backs on their own culture, give up what they believe, defy program policies, or disregard the mandates of regulating agencies.[2] We are simply asking that they question the common assumption that there is one right way to do things, recognizing instead that other ways of believing may also have merit. We believe that when families and early childhood professionals approach their relationship with the desire to learn from one another, wonderful transformations can take place. It is those transformations that are the vision behind our work.

[2]Some cultural practices are, of course, not permissible in the United States. Being open to other cultural perspectives does not mean allowing a child to be harmed or laws to be broken. Early childhood professionals are trained to recognize possible threats to a child's health and well-being; cultural knowledge can be useful in understanding parents' views of particular behaviors (their children's, their own, program staff's) and fostering communication when a conflict occurs.

Validity of the Framework and the BC–ECE Module

The Bridging Cultures framework is based on theory and research about individualism and collectivism (see collected articles in Rogoff, 2003; Rothstein-Fisch, 2003b; Shweder et al., 1998). These concepts have been useful in understanding the cultural values of families with Native American roots, African roots, and Asian roots (Greenfield, 1994). Research about miscommunication during parent–teacher conferences (Greenfield et al., 2000) show how beliefs associated with individualism and collectivism are often in opposition and can lead to confusion and misunderstanding between those who hold differing beliefs.

The BC–ECE module was field tested in three venues with four groups representing all of the target groups for whom the module was developed. Feedback was solicited from all participants (see Appendix E for a summary), and after each presentation, improvements were made to the module based on the feedback.

Caution: Culture Is Complex

When thinking about cultural diversity, it is important to keep several things in mind.

The framework describes a culture's orientation, not an individual's orientation. Most people have a combination of individualistic and collectivistic qualities; therefore, we caution against making broad generalizations or forming quick impressions about people. There is much diversity in every culture and every individual. In fact, many people identify themselves as bicultural or multicultural. It will always be important to watch, listen, and respectfully ask questions to understand the cultural priorities of any child or family.

A variety of factors influence a family's relative orientation toward collectivism or individualism. Does the family come from an urban or rural background? What type of schooling did the parents and grandparents receive in their home country? Are family members monolingual or bilingual (or multilingual)?[3] Therefore, to understand a family, it is important to consider not just its country of origin or background but also other aspects of its history.

Cultures change when they come in contact with other influences. Although a shift away from collectivistic values toward individualistic values often comes with greater access to education or a move to an urban environment, essential values tend to be maintained across many generations, even after immigration to a country that has a dominant culture with a different value system. Urban dwellers who have had access to higher education and a good income, whose family roots are in Mexico or Japan or South America, for example, are still likely to be much more collectivistic than European Americans (cf. Greenfield & Cocking, 1994).

The culture of any group is affected by how its members are viewed by other groups based, in part, on their racial and ethnic identity. The Bridging Cultures approach is not intended to downplay the importance of race and ethnicity in people's experience. In fact, it is designed to complement antibias and antiracist educational efforts (cf. Derman-Sparks & Phillips, 1997). Culture can be a common denominator across racial and ethnic groups, but it's also true that members of the same racial or ethnic group may have very different cultural values. (One might think of differences between African Americans and recent immigrants to the United States from sub-Saharan African nations.) Bridging

[3]Maintenance of one's language of origin may be associated with maintenance of cultural values.

Cultures training can be an excellent starting place for understanding human differences because, with greater cultural understanding, it may be easier to tackle issues of racism, power differences, and inequity.

Finally, some people worry that we are doing a disservice by reducing something as complex as culture to a single framework. We know it's not as simple as the old saying, "There are two kinds of people in the world." We know that having some knowledge of a person's culture doesn't mean you can predict that person's behavior. And we know that human experience is too rich to fit neatly into any conceptual scheme, that no society is completely collectivistic or individualistic. Therefore, our point is not to stereotype people by putting them into boxes but rather to use the concepts of individualism and collectivism to help early childhood professionals understand that in many families, culture-based priorities differ from those of the "mainstream."

We hope that what follows is not only interesting but also useful and productive for both facilitators and workshop participants. We hope it spawns new ways of thinking and interacting that bring people together for the common purpose of successfully caring for and educating infants, toddlers, and young children from all backgrounds.

Chapter 2

Facilitator's Script

Overview

This chapter offers a script designed to guide a presentation of the concepts and ideas underlying BC–ECE. The script is intended for a 2-hour workshop in which participants explore the differences between two contrasting value systems—individualism and collectivism. Examples relevant to early childhood settings are used throughout to illustrate these two value systems. Because of the amount of information presented, we advise that the module not be attempted in less than 2 hours.

It is not necessary to follow the script word for word. In fact, experienced presenters may be comfortable adapting the material without use of the script. But we advise that, before their first workshop, all presenters consider the suggestions contained in Appendix D. These include recommendations about the best use of the module and about approaches to understanding cultural differences. Also discussed in Appendix D are two essential elements in any successful workshop related to diversity: time and trust. It takes time to digest the framework, and if people are to engage in the self-exploration necessary for deep engagement in this work, they must feel secure, trusting that the facilitator and their fellow participants will support them, not judge them. Professionals who work with diversity issues know that the topic of cultural differences may spark debate and elicit differences of opinion among participants. It is important to have strategies for ensuring that differences are expressed and received in a constructive manner. Finally, Appendix D includes a brief discussion of how to accommodate different learning strengths and suggestions for organizing the presentation itself, such as the preparation of materials and the environment.

It should be noted that the script for this training module does not include a break, but facilitators are encouraged to insert one where they see fit. Remember that additional suggestions for expanding the learning are described in chapter 3.

Professional Development Objectives

In this workshop participants will begin to:

- Recognize contrasting cultural patterns in the care and education of young children
- Reflect on personal values and values implicit in program practices
- Expand definitions of culturally responsive care and education
- Consider new ways to promote equity in early childhood care and education

Guide to Using the Script

There are two parts to the script: On the inside of the page is the script itself, proposed language for the facilitator; on the outside are notes for the facilitator.

At the start of each new section in the script column, a bulleted list of key concepts and experiences cues the facilitator to what follows. As mentioned earlier, facilitators should feel free to use their own words to express some of the concepts and ideas of this module. We recommend, however, that presenters highlight key parts of the script they might want to read to participants word for word for purposes of clarity and accuracy. They may especially want to note important questions that are asked of participants for each activity. Facilitators should also feel free to augment the script by relating relevant personal experiences.

The "notes" column contains facilitator instructions along with other useful information, such as how participants might be expected to respond to certain questions or when to anticipate participant confusion. The notes can help facilitators plan how best to present key concepts and organize activities for their group. Facilitators are also encouraged to write their own comments in that space, for example, to remind themselves of additional activities they might want to use, perhaps drawing from those described in chapter 3. Each time we have used the module, we have learned from our participants and incorporated their experiences into our own thinking. The notes are a good place to keep a record of such learning and teaching moments for later use.

In the notes, a small icon of a hand signals when to give participants a handout; an asterisk * signifies when to put up an overhead.

SCRIPT	NOTES

Key Concepts/Experiences

- **Help participants identify their own experiences with cultural conflict.**
- **Establish objectives for the workshop.**

How many of you have ever found yourself thinking, "Gee, *why* does that mother do *that* with her child?" In other words, have you ever been challenged by parenting practices that may conflict with your own ideas or assumptions about good childrearing? Or, have you ever found yourself disagreeing with your program's policy about something like feeding, separation, or use of toys? Let's see a show of hands. Who has ever felt the tug of cultural conflict or confusion?

Today I am going to share some ideas that can help explain "why" each of us does things in a certain way and why other people might do them differently. Understanding these differences and what's behind them can help us bridge them, making your job easier. Building such bridges can also make the families you serve feel more comfortable in your program, which, in turn, may lead them to be more involved. When parents are involved with those who care for and educate their child, everyone benefits—the child, the family, and the program.

Let's spend a moment to become acquainted. By a show of hands, how many of you are early childhood teachers?

How many work with children 3 to 5 years of age? How many work with children under 3? How many are family child-care providers?

Introduction of Participants

Introductions are only necessary when the workshop is conducted for people who do not already know each other; they are unnecessary in an ongoing course, such as at a community college.

NOTES

SCRIPT

Introduction of Workshop Facilitator(s)

If the module is not part of a course, where everyone knows each other, introduce yourself briefly, along with any cofacilitators.

Home visitors? Early interventionists? Parent educators? How many are program administrators? Any primary school teachers here? What other kinds of jobs are represented?

Put up **Overhead 1:** Professional Development Objectives.

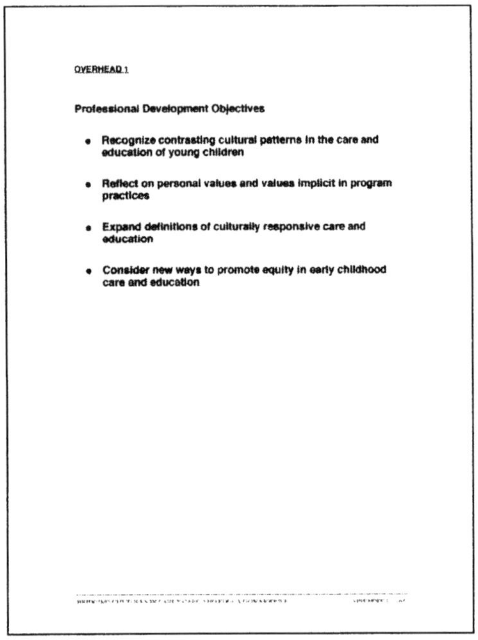

OVERHEAD 1

Professional Development Objectives

- Recognize contrasting cultural patterns in the care and education of young children
- Reflect on personal values and values implicit in program practices
- Expand definitions of culturally responsive care and education
- Consider new ways to promote equity in early childhood care and education

In this workshop you will begin to

- Recognize contrasting cultural patterns in the care and education of young children
- Reflect on personal values and values implicit in program practices
- Expand definitions of culturally responsive care and education
- Consider new ways to promote equity in early childhood care and education

SCRIPT

Here's what is planned:

- **Contrasting Approaches**

  Activity 1: Contrasting Approaches to Feeding

- **Building a Framework: Individualism and Collectivism**

  Activity 2: Thinking in terms of patterns: Individual Orientation and Group Orientation

  Activity 3: Exploring patterns in practice

  Activity 4: Self-reflection: Where do you fit?

  Activity 5: Thinking about your workplace

  Activity 6: Proverbs (optional)

  Activity 7: Further exploration of patterns (optional)

- **Reflection**

  Activity 8: Wrap-up (optional)

- **Evaluation**

  Activity 9: Comments about workshop

NOTES

Put up **Overhead 2:** Module Agenda.

OVERHEAD 2

Module Agenda

- **Contrasting Approaches**

  Activity 1: Contrasting approaches to feeding

- **Building a Framework: Individualism and collectivism**

  Activity 2: Thinking in terms of patterns: Individual orientation and group orientation

  Activity 3: Exploring patterns in practice

  Activity 4: Self-reflection: Where do you fit?

  Activity 5: Thinking about your workplace

  Activity 6: Proverbs (optional)

  Activity 7: Further exploration of patterns (optional)

- **Reflection**

  Activity 8: Wrap-up (optional)

- **Evaluation**

  Activity 9: Comments about workshop

NOTES

Distribute **Handout 1:** How Two Mothers Feed Their Children.

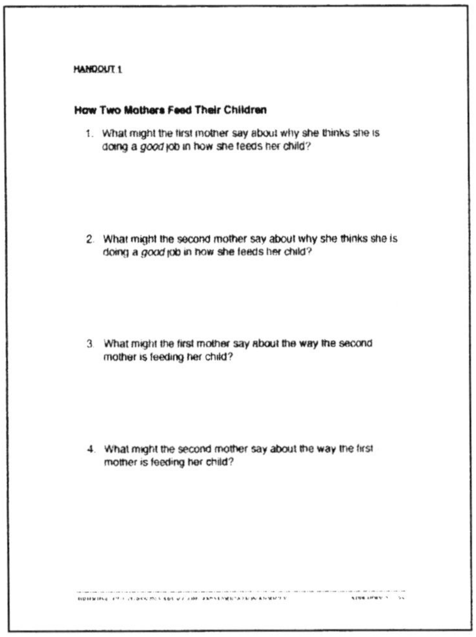

HANDOUT 1

How Two Mothers Feed Their Children

1. What might the first mother say about why she thinks she is doing a *good* job in how she feeds her child?

2. What might the second mother say about why she thinks she is doing a *good* job in how she feeds her child?

3. What might the first mother say about the way the second mother is feeding her child?

4. What might the second mother say about the way the first mother is feeding her child?

SCRIPT

ACTIVITY 1

Contrasting Approaches to Feeding

Time: 15 minutes

Key Concepts/Experiences

- **Introduce activity by showing overhead of baby in highchair.**
- **Ask questions and get feedback.**
- **Share additional responses.**
- **Show overhead of mother spoon-feeding her child.**
- **Ask questions and get feedback.**

SCRIPT

We're going to look at two approaches to feeding young children. This is the way one mother, Mother 1, feeds her child. Although you do not see the mother in the photograph, she is off to one side attending to some other tasks in the kitchen. She is keeping an eye on the infant and talking to him while she works in the kitchen.

What might this mother say about why she thinks she is doing a *good* job in how she feeds her child? Please look at Handout 1 and think about it, perhaps jotting down some ideas.

NOTES

Put up **Overhead 3:** Baby in High Chair.

Depending on your group, you may want to give names to the mother and child pictured in each overhead, to help participants keep the two feeding scenarios clear during discussion. Remember, however, that names often imply a certain ethnic or racial identity. Gauge your participants to determine if adding a name to the mother or child in each scenario would help or hinder participants' understanding and discussion. After participants think about or write down their own ideas, initiate a large-group discussion. Write people's responses on a blank overhead, flipchart, or whiteboard.

Possible responses to the question of what the mother might be thinking are:

1. Exploring is desirable and the child is exploring the food.
2. Children need to learn how to eat by themselves and develop a variety of self-help skills.

NOTES

3. Children have to try out new things in their own way.
4. Feeding this way helps the child gain independence or autonomy.
5. The child is developing small motor skills and/or eye–hand coordination.
6. The child is having a sensory experience.
7. Eating this way helps the child develop self-confidence.

✳ Put up **Overhead 4:** Mother Spoon-Feeding Her Preschooler.

SCRIPT

Here is another feeding scene. What might this mother, Mother 2, say about why she thinks she is doing a good job in how she feeds her child? Use Handout 1 to think about or write your ideas.

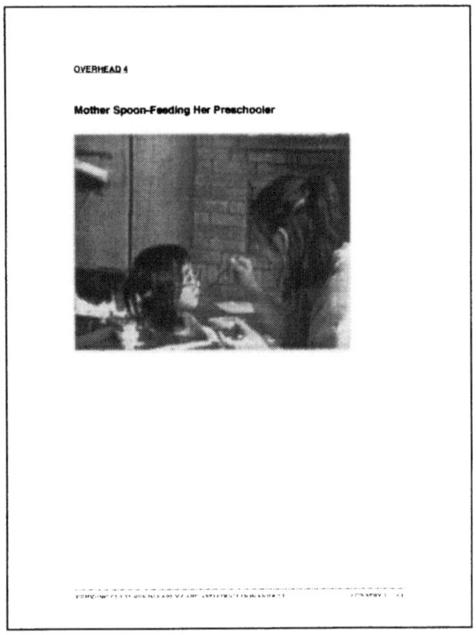

Some might respond to the image of the mother spoon-feeding her child by asking whether the child is developmentally disabled or delayed, whether she has special needs. The answer is no. The question of special needs is likely to be brought up by a participant who assumes that a parent would *only* use this feeding method if the child could not possibly feed herself.

SCRIPT

NOTES

This assumption reflects a more individualistic response: Learning to feed oneself is assumed to be the goal. The feeding style in this example is more closely based on collectivistic notions, demonstrating that the mother and child are engaged in a helping-and-being-helped dynamic, valued for establishing that relationship.

Possible responses to the question of what the mother might be thinking are:

1. She's helping her child and that tells the child her mother cares about her.
2. Feeding her child ensures that the child gets proper nutrition/food.
3. It's important to foster obedience or manners.
4. The mother is in control and can avoid a mess, keeping her kitchen clean.
5. Feeding is a way to develop a closer relationship with her child.
6. She is taking care of her child's needs.
7. The child is learning to be helped so she can help others later on.
8. She is not wasting food.

Key Concepts/Experiences

- **Ask participants to speculate about what the two mothers might say about each other.**
- **Make the point that, generally speaking, there are no absolutes when it comes to feeding. There's more than one right way, depending on the perspective.**

What might the first mother, the one whose child is feeding himself, think about the second mother's way of feeding her child?

Think about or write your thoughts on Handout 1.

Possible responses regarding what the first mother might be thinking about how the second mother is feeding her child include:

1. The mother is not letting her child be independent.
2. She is babying her child, spoiling her.
3. She is too controlling, not allowing choices, and is overprotective.
4. The child won't develop important motor skills.

NOTES

5. There must be something wrong with the child because the mother must feed her.
6. The mother is insecure and needs the child to be dependent on her.

Possible responses include:

1. She doesn't care about her child; she lacks devotion.
2. She is too busy to help the child.
3. She is too permissive, allowing the child too much freedom.
4. This child is making a mess and may not be eating enough.
5. The child is wasting food.
6. The mother doesn't give her child enough attention; there may not be a loving relationship as would be demonstrated by helping.

Encourage participants to focus on how the different feeding approaches are imparting different ideas to the children. In the first case, the mother values independence and may want to teach the child to eat by himself. This mother believes her child should be allowed to explore his food and doesn't mind if he gets messy. In the second case, the mother may believe that she is a caring and conscientious mother because she is helping her child eat. She may also want to teach her child to accept her mother's help.

SCRIPT

Think about or jot down your thoughts about what the second mother, the one who is spoon-feeding her child, might think about the first mother's method of feeding her child?

Although you may have strong feelings about one method of feeding being more appropriate than the other, there are a variety of ways to feed a child.

Key Concepts/Experiences

- **Feeding practices are based on values.**
- **The two feeding scenes demonstrate individualism and collectivism, respectively.**
- **Individualism focuses on becoming independent.**
- **Collectivism focuses on developing interdependent relationships within the family or group.**

Feeding methods, like all aspects of caregiving and education, reflect values.

SCRIPT	NOTES

You might say that the mother in the first photo values the need of the *individual* child to become *independent. She wants the child to be free to explore and gain mastery of self-feeding.* You might say that the second mother is trying to foster a sense of *interdependence*. She wants the child to learn how to accept and give help in the context of a mutually supportive *relationship*. Thinking about these two value orientations—fostering the value of the individual or, in contrast, the value of the relationship—is the objective of this workshop.

Let's look at another example:

All About Me

Put up **Overhead 5:** All About Me.

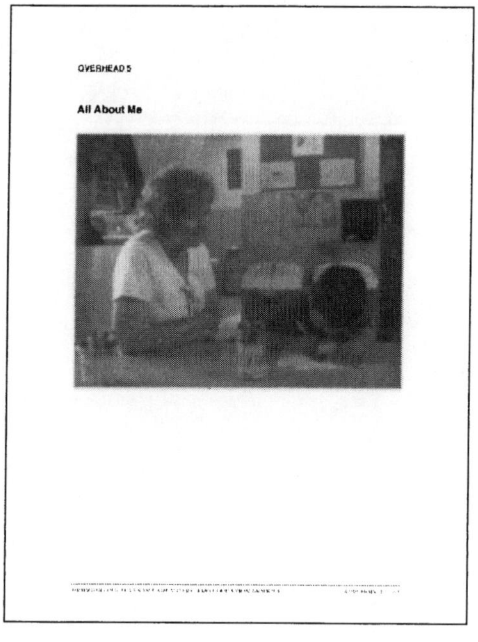

Each child in the preschool group is making a book called *All About Me*. The teacher asks each one to say what is special about himself or herself. The teacher writes the comment and the child draws a picture to go with the words. One boy responds to the question with examples about other people: His brother is very good at soccer and his father is very good at cooking. The teacher keeps asking the boy to describe qualities about himself, prompting him by saying, "This is all about you. Are you smart? Yes, of course you are, so let's say you are special because you are smart." In the end, the boy's book contains drawings with dictated sentences such as "I am special because I am strong; and I am special because I am smart, and I am special because I am handsome."

When the boy's mother sees the book, she looks distressed instead of delighted, as the teacher had expected.

Read the scenario aloud.

NOTES

Provide participants with **Handout 2:** All About Me.

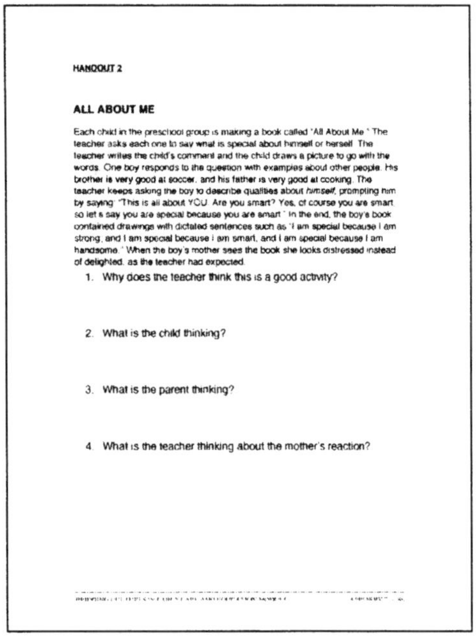

HANDOUT 2

ALL ABOUT ME

Each child in the preschool group is making a book called "All About Me." The teacher asks each one to say what is special about himself or herself. The teacher writes the child's comment and the child draws a picture to go with the words. One boy responds to the question with examples about other people. His brother is very good at soccer, and his father is very good at cooking. The teacher keeps asking the boy to describe qualities about *himself*, prompting him by saying: "This is all about YOU. Are you smart? Yes, of course you are smart, so let's say you are special because you are smart." In the end, the boy's book contained drawings with dictated sentences such as "I am special because I am strong, and I am special because I am smart, and I am special because I am handsome." When the boy's mother sees the book she looks distressed instead of delighted, as the teacher had expected.

1. Why does the teacher think this is a good activity?
2. What is the child thinking?
3. What is the parent thinking?
4. What is the teacher thinking about the mother's reaction?

This activity can be conducted as a whole-group activity where responses are noted on a flipchart or an overhead transparency; it can also be discussed in smaller groups or in pairs.

Possible answers might include:

1. An emphasis on the object versus the person (an off-target response).
2. Miscommunication or misunderstanding.
3. The child is not used to self-praise and needs encouragement.

SCRIPT

Why do you think the mother looked upset?

Look at Handout 2.

What do you think is going on? Think about or, if you would like, write down the first thing that comes to you. Your answers don't have to be long.

Turn to someone nearby and discuss your answers to the questions. You have 10 minutes.

During your discussion, did you sense that there may have been some tension between the teacher's desire to focus on the child as an individual, and the child's and mother's need to see the boy as part of his family, as a member of a group?

In the case of the *All About Me* book, what kinds of conflict did you notice between the focus on the individual and the focus on the family?

SCRIPT	NOTES
	4. A conflict in beliefs—the teacher wants the child to respond to her beliefs. 5. The teacher doesn't know much about the child's culture. 6. The teacher's perspective of what's special versus the child's perspective. 7. The child tries to please the teacher.
Why does the teacher think this is a good activity?	Possible responses might include: 1. The teacher wants the child to see himself as a unique individual. 2. The teacher thinks, "I need to get these books done before Open House, so I'll help the child finish his book." 3. The little boy doesn't understand the language or can't express himself, so she wants to help him. 4. The teacher wants to promote positive self-esteem.
What is the child thinking?	Possible answers to what the child is thinking might include: 1. I'm confused; maybe my thoughts don't count and my words aren't valued. 2. Is this what my teacher thinks of me and how she would describe me? 3. I don't want to brag, but she is making me do it. 4. Maybe my family is not as important as I thought, or maybe my teacher doesn't like my family. 5. I'm uncomfortable sticking out from the rest of the family and wanted to focus on my whole family, so I won't be selfish.
What is the parent thinking?	Possible answers to what the parent is thinking might include: 1. Why is my son bragging about himself? 2. My son wouldn't say that! 3. Will my son become self-centered and boastful? Will he separate himself from the family?

NOTES

4. How did that teacher get her job?
5. Should I just take my son home?
6. My child is not showing modesty or humility.

Possible answers about what the teacher might be thinking include:

1. The mother doesn't care for her son's feelings or thoughts.
2. Why doesn't the mother want her son to have a positive self-esteem?

SCRIPT

What is the teacher thinking about the mother's reaction?

ACTIVITY 2

Thinking in Terms of Patterns: Individual Orientation and Group Orientation

Time: 15 minutes

Key Concepts/Experiences

- **Values can be organized with a framework of individualism and collectivism as a way of understanding cultural differences.**
- **Define individualism and collectivism.**
- **Demonstrate how the framework of individualism and collectivism fit the feeding and All About Me examples.**
- **Show and review chart.**

In each of the examples we have shared, we can see a pattern of thinking about the "ideal child." The goals for children are based on beliefs called "cultural values orientations" and they often center on the needs of the individual versus the needs of the group.

SCRIPT	NOTES

In the first example, the mother of the child sitting in the highchair allows her child to become messy as an exploration of food or because she hopes that the child will learn how to self-feed. In the second photo, the mother helps her child learn that families depend on each other and that receiving and giving help to others is very important.

Similar contrasting values orientations are also evident in the second example, All About Me. The teacher may be trying to develop the boy's positive self-esteem by having him showcase his individual strengths or talents. But the child is confused, and when the mother sees her son's book, she views him as being self-centered. In her view, he should have been thinking of and representing himself as part of a group, in this case, his family.

These differing orientations can affect all kinds of expectations and behavior, from how children use toys to how early childhood professionals organize learning environments.

Let's look at a chart that begins to organize these two different ways of thinking about the world. Here, in the individual orientation, you can see that the primary focus is on the individual functioning independently. In the group orientation, you can see that the primary focus is on functioning within a group.

Put up **Overhead 6:** Chart of Individual and Group Orientation.

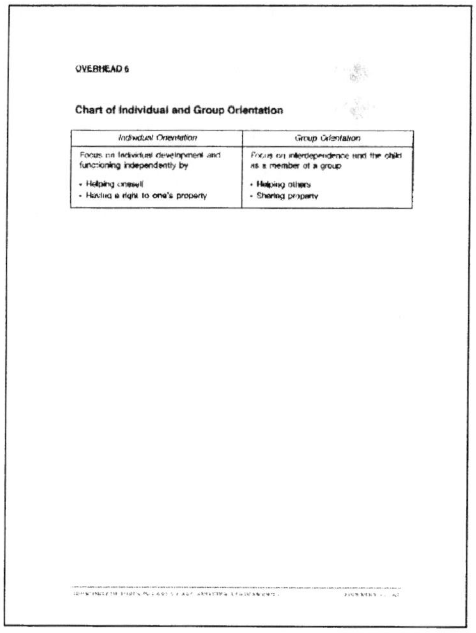
OVERHEAD 6

Chart of Individual and Group Orientation

Individual Orientation	*Group Orientation*
Focus on individual development and functioning independently by • Helping oneself • Having a right to one's property	Focus on interdependence and the child as a member of a group • Helping others • Sharing property

NOTES

Put up **Overhead 7:** Greenfield Quotation.

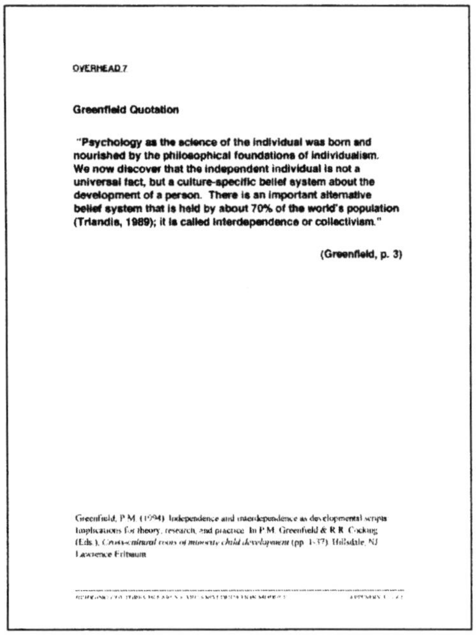
OVERHEAD 7

Greenfield Quotation

"Psychology as the science of the individual was born and nourished by the philosophical foundations of individualism. We now discover that the independent individual is not a universal fact, but a culture-specific belief system about the development of a person. There is an important alternative belief system that is held by about 70% of the world's population (Triandis, 1989); it is called interdependence or collectivism."

(Greenfield, p. 3)

Greenfield, P. M. (1994). Independence and interdependence as developmental scripts: Implications for theory, research, and practice. In P. M. Greenfield & R. R. Cocking (Eds.), *Cross-cultural roots of minority child development* (pp. 1-37). Hillsdale, NJ: Lawrence Erlbaum.

SCRIPT

Key Concept

- **Psychology is based on the development of the individual.**

Let's take a look at a quotation about how psychology has focused on the idea of individual development. This quotation is from Patricia Greenfield, one of the developers of the Bridging Cultures framework. Here, she notes that the majority of the world's people do not hold to the individualistic orientation.

SCRIPT

Key Concepts/Experiences

- **Hofstede (2001) identified differences in individualism across various countries.**
- **Seventy percent of the world's countries could be categorized as collectivistic.**

Over 35 years ago, social psychologist Geert Hofstede studied individualism in 72 countries as part of a study about workers for a large corporation. You might be interested to know about the relative focus on individualism in your family's background. Here is a short list of some of the countries he studied.

Notice that Hofstede was interested in individualism, not collectivism per se, so collectivism was measured relative to the amount of individualism. He found that 70% of the countries he studied could be categorized as collectivistic, not individualistic. However, as you can see from the list, the United States, Australia, Great Britain, and Canada each scored high on the individualism ratings.

NOTES

Put up **Overhead 8:** Hofstede's Individualism Ratings.

OVERHEAD 8

Hofstede's Individualism Ratings

USA	91
Australia	90
Great Britain	89
Canada	80
Italy	76
France, Sweden	71
Germany	67
Israel	54
Spain	51
India	48
Argentina, Japan	47
Iran	41
"Arab countries," Brazil	38
Philippines	32
Mexico	30
Hong Kong	25
Singapore, Thailand	20
"West African countries"	20
South Korea	18
Costa Rica	15
Indonesia, Pakistan	14
Guatemala	6

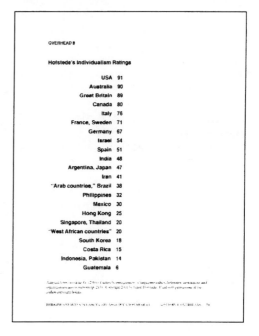

For those who do not see the country they are interested in, there is a full list of the countries studied by Hofstede (2001) in Appendix C.

An important underlying concept here is not to view a high rating as good and a low rating as bad, or vice versa; rather, the intent is to help people understand that nationality contributes to people's value systems. Our value system or orientation informs us about what we think is good for children.

An interesting contrast of individualism and collectivism is illustrated in the childrearing practice of sleeping arrangements for infants. Sleeping arrangements are related to expectations about whether infants should be allowed to settle themselves to sleep or be helped to sleep through touching and soothing caregiving behavior. Morelli, Rogoff, Oppenheim, and

NOTES

Goldsmith (1992) contrasted the infant sleeping practices of Mayan parents in Guatemala with the infant sleeping practices of middle-class Anglos in the United States.[1] All the Mayan mothers in this study had their infants sleep next to them because they were concerned about their health and safety. When Mayan mothers were told of the U.S. practice of having infants sleep apart from their parents, they expressed concern and offered sympathy for the U.S. infants.

An individualistic orientation will conflict with the collectivistic values that many immigrants bring from their homelands in Asia, Latin America, and Africa. The individualistic orientation will also pose conflicts for other groups who often have strong ties to their collectivistic culture of origin, for example, Native Americans and, to some degree, African Americans.

Observe the audience for signs that participants understand what is being presented.

SCRIPT

Key Concepts/Experiences

- **Individualism is not universal.**
- **Changing practices to adjust to cultural differences may result in conflict with established rules and regulations.**

The two examples we discussed, feeding and making a book *All About Me*, show us that there are different ideas about what is important for children to learn in order to function in their family and in the culture to which the family belongs. Mainstream U.S. culture is the most individualistic in the world but, as we have noted, individualism is not universal. So, the question for us is how to reconcile the differences between collectivism and individualism to best help children and families.

According to National Association for the Education of Young Children (NAEYC) and Head Start guidelines, early childhood educators are responsible for making adaptations to programs to meet diversity needs. Yet trying to be culturally responsive can present all kinds of problems because policies, regulations, standards, and, in many cases, a teacher's own training may not take collectivistic or group orientations into consideration.

[1]See Morelli et al. (1992). Also see how sleeping and feeding arrangements are affected by parental goals in Greenfield and Suzuki (1998).

SCRIPT	NOTES
A collectivistic approach is often dismissed as the "wrong" way to do things, or seen as impeding children's independence, though we now know that the goal of independence is hardly universal.	
What happens when a family's culture-based beliefs are different from the beliefs guiding your program practices or different from your own beliefs?	
Key Concepts/Experiences	
• **No one culture (or person) is completely individualistic or collectivistic. Personal histories are important in shaping these differences between people.** • **Some people have incorporated both value orientations and consider themselves bicultural.**	
Before sharing other examples of cultural differences and their possible impact, I'm going to say a few words about the overgeneralization of categories.	
Some cultural groups are much more group oriented than others, but does this mean that everyone from that culture believes the same way?	Throughout this section, questions are posed to the whole group. Wait for participants to nod heads; if needed, paraphrase the question to elicit some indication that they understand there is variation even within a culture.
Knowing the patterns of how people have adapted to life in various cultures is helpful in trying to understand not only other people's cultural values but our own as well.	

NOTES	SCRIPT

Many people are bicultural: Some have parents from two different cultures. Others may have parents who were born in another country but may, themselves, have been born or raised in the United States. Some may have become somewhat bicultural by marrying someone from a culture different from their own or by growing up in a neighborhood where they had strong interactions with individuals from other cultures.

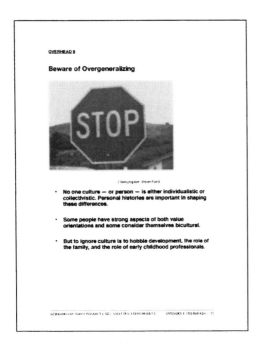

✱ Put up **Overhead 9:** Beware of Overgeneralizing.

OVERHEAD 9

Beware of Overgeneralizing

- No one culture — or person — is either individualistic or collectivistic. Personal histories are important in shaping these differences.
- Some people have strong aspects of both value orientations and some consider themselves bicultural.
- But to ignore culture is to hobble development, the role of the family, and the role of early childhood professionals.

Raise your hand if you consider yourself bicultural.

How many of you have ever experienced conflict between what your parents told you and what teachers or schools taught you? Sometimes it is hard to figure out exactly how to deal with cultural differences, but understanding the "why" behind people's actions and responses can help.

Optional exercise: Participants can discuss in a small group or write down an example of a conflict they observed or experienced.

SCRIPT	NOTES

Key Concepts/Experiences

- **Understanding the "why" of people's behavior may help us figure out what might be done to resolve conflicts.**
- **How can we make culture "visible"?**

Part of the challenge in resolving conflicts based on cultural differences is that the real source of the conflict is often invisible. All we see is the behavior. Because our own cultural values are so pervasive and ingrained, we're often not even *aware* of our culture or of how it affects us. People have said it's like being a fish in the water: The fish doesn't notice the water because it has never been in any other environment. What I am trying to do through the examples I share with you is to make the invisible visible—to reveal the "why" behind the behavior.

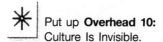

Put up **Overhead 10:** Culture Is Invisible.

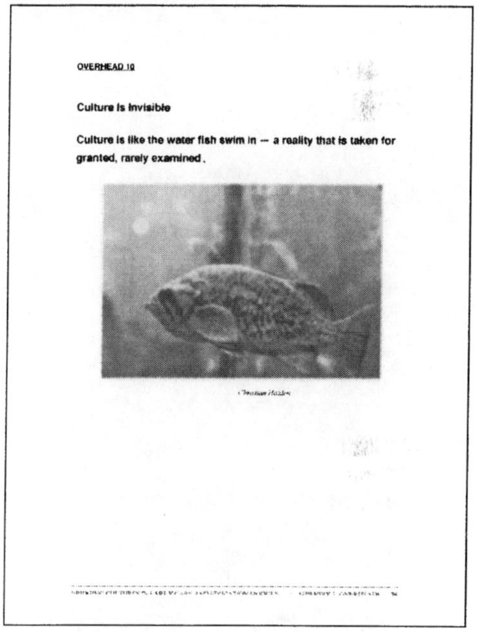

Practitioners, caregivers, and teachers who have used the framework of individualism and collectivism have experienced how understanding *why* a conflict is occurring can make it less disturbing.

Understanding the reasons for people's behavior may or may not change our own behavior, but it is certainly a first step toward reducing or resolving conflict. And, in some instances, better understanding of cultural issues may help us anticipate a potential conflict and avoid it altogether.

Optional exercise: Have participants work in pairs and identify an experience in their work where they thought that individualistic and collectivistic orientations were in conflict with each other. What was the conflict? Was it resolved? How?

Was anybody's behavior changed as a result of the conflict?

NOTES

SCRIPT

Block Example

Time: 15 minutes

Key Concepts/Experiences

- **Construct a chart that organizes responses into individualistic versus collectivistic.**
- **An individualistic orientation would assume that the child who played with blocks first is entitled to them.**
- **The group or collectivistic orientation sees the blocks as communal property for all children.**

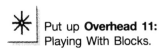

Put up **Overhead 11:** Playing With Blocks.

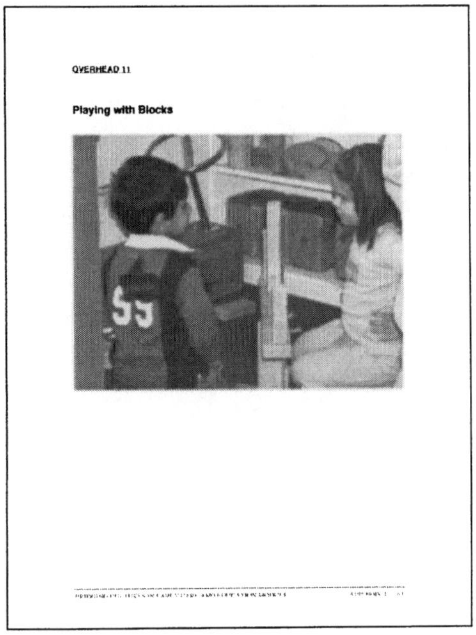

Let's consider another example of conflict and see if our model of individualism versus collectivism helps us understand it.

Picture this: At preschool, a girl is playing with blocks. A boy who is playing nearby takes one of the blocks that the girl is not using. The girl protests, saying, "That's mine!" The teacher comes over and says to the boy, "Now, she used her words to tell you that's her block. You need to listen to her and ask permission if you want to use it." The boy's mother is in another part of the room, and a look of shock is on her face at the way the teacher handled the incident.

In a small group of three to four people, spend 10 minutes discussing what is happening here:

> What might the boy be thinking or feeling? What cultural value orientation—individualism or collectivism—motivates his behavior?
>
> What might the girl be thinking or feeling? What is her cultural value orientation?

SCRIPT

What values does the teacher seem to hold? What things seem most important to her?

What is the boy's mother thinking or feeling? What might her values be?

Let's see what ideas came up in the discussion, and we'll construct a chart to see which ideas fall more into the individual orientation and which ideas reflect a more collectivistic or group orientation. There may be some ideas that don't fit in either category.

In this scenario, the notion of property rights is addressed. Whose property are the blocks? Do they belong to the children as a group, or to the individual child who happens to be playing with them?

NOTES

Provide **Handout 3:** Playing With Blocks.

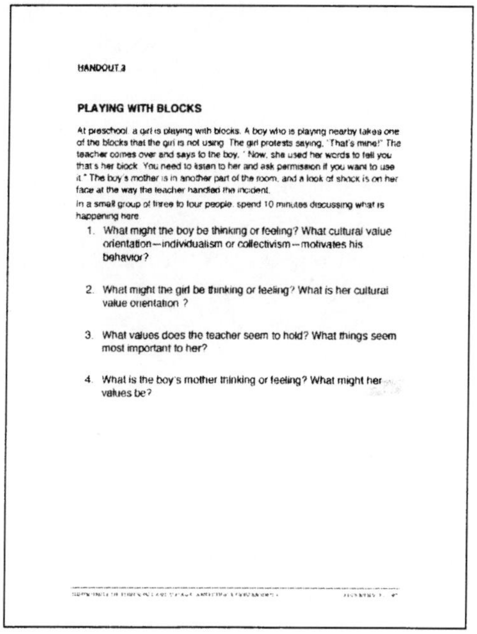

HANDOUT 3

PLAYING WITH BLOCKS

At preschool, a girl is playing with blocks. A boy who is playing nearby takes one of the blocks that the girl is not using. The girl protests saying, "That's mine!" The teacher comes over and says to the boy, "Now, she used her words to tell you that's her block. You need to listen to her and ask permission if you want to use it." The boy's mother is in another part of the room, and a look of shock is on her face at the way the teacher handled the incident.

In a small group of three to four people, spend 10 minutes discussing what is happening here.

1. What might the boy be thinking or feeling? What cultural value orientation—individualism or collectivism—motivates his behavior?
2. What might the girl be thinking or feeling? What is her cultural value orientation ?
3. What values does the teacher seem to hold? What things seem most important to her?
4. What is the boy's mother thinking or feeling? What might her values be?

After 9 minutes, see if the groups are finished. (If not, let them know how much time they have left.) In the meantime, circulate to see if the participants are on track and discussing the issues of property, or of group versus the individual.

Responses to the question of property rules at school might prompt a side discussion of how different teachers or caregivers foster sharing. Responses might include, "In my program we . . .

1. take turns, telling children, 'I'll give you five minutes then you have to share.' "
2. honor the child playing, and teach others to be patient."
3. all play together, and if there is an argument over a toy, we watch the children solve it themselves."

These are all individualistic responses.

NOTES	SCRIPT

Teachers may also mention the child's developmental level and the child's ability to understand and respond to particular expectations.

People with different cultural orientations may have different ideas about property rights. Those with an individualistic orientation may view this situation as one where the child who had the blocks first has the right to play with them alone, and if another child wants to use them, he has to make a request. The girl doesn't "own" them, but she has the right of access because she chose first.

Put up **Overhead 12:** Blank Chart of Individualism and Collectivism.

Those with a collectivistic orientation might view this situation (as the mother did) as one where property is to be shared by all. How might we put this on our chart?

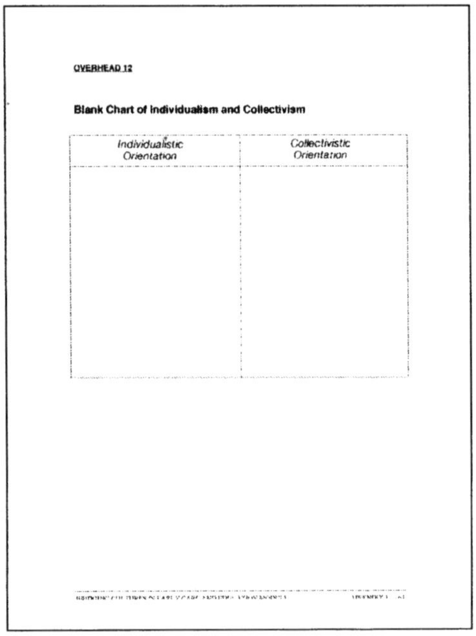

Invite people to share their thoughts about the block-play conflict, beginning with the notion of property. On a blank transparency, or a flipchart, write down the comments made by participants. Then go over all the comments and see if they can be organized into the framework.

SCRIPT | NOTES

Here is what a representative chart might look like, but be sure to honor the ideas of the group even if the chart doesn't come out like the following chart:

Individualistic Orientation	*Collectivistic Orientation*
Choice to share	Share automatically
Ask permission to use objects because they "temporarily" belong to the other child	Objects belong to the group; teacher should be helping children share
Using words to communicate	Using observation to learn with the focus on others
Teacher sided with the girl	Mother felt that her son was being discriminated against

This scenario was taken from a real preschool incident. The real case was even more dramatic because the first child playing with the blocks hit the other child and the teacher scolded the crying child for taking blocks that "belonged" to someone else.

You may want to acknowledge that this is a somewhat extreme example: All preschools expect children to share; nevertheless, unless a special request is made (and she chooses to share), the girl's "individual right to the blocks" is an underlying assumption and is probably not uncommon.

The blocks belong to the school, and the perceived "ownership" by the child is at best only temporary. Yet, if children assume the blocks belong to the group and they are for everyone, then "asking permission" to play with them seems absurd from a collectivistic perspective, particularly for those who come from homes where possessions are routinely and automatically shared.

Once you have recorded all the initial answers, add to the framework on the overhead those that seem most pertinent. Do not feel compelled to add all the information from the preceding list, but do suggest these as possible responses if it seems appropriate given time and group readiness.

For a detailed description of the actual incident, see Trumbull, Greenfield, and Quiroz (2004).

NOTES

Put up **Overhead 13:** First Thing in the Morning.

OVERHEAD 13

First Thing in the Morning

Pass out **Handout 4:** First Thing in the Morning.

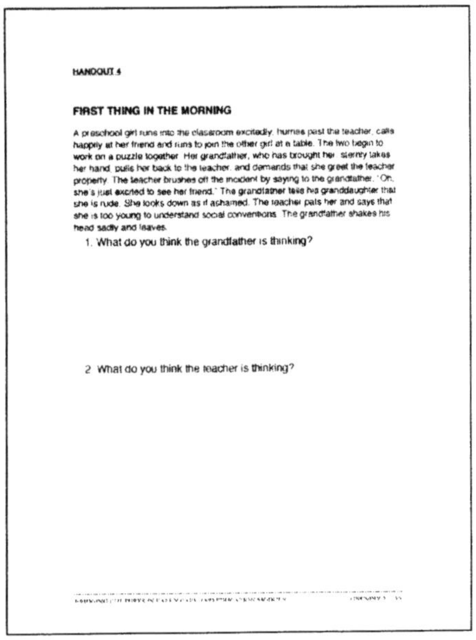
HANDOUT 4

FIRST THING IN THE MORNING

A preschool girl runs into the classroom excitedly, hurries past the teacher, calls happily at her friend and runs to join the other girl at a table. The two begin to work on a puzzle together. Her grandfather, who has brought her, sternly takes her hand, pulls her back to the teacher, and demands that she greet the teacher properly. The teacher brushes off the incident by saying to the grandfather, "Oh, she's just excited to see her friend." The grandfather tells his granddaughter that she is rude. She looks down as if ashamed. The teacher pats her and says that she is too young to understand social conventions. The grandfather shakes his head sadly and leaves.

1. What do you think the grandfather is thinking?

2. What do you think the teacher is thinking?

SCRIPT

ACTIVITY 3

Exploring Patterns in Practice

Time: 15 minutes

Key Concepts/Experiences

- **An individualistic orientation would assume that it is permissible for a preschool child to greet people in the order in which they wish.**
- **A collectivistic orientation assumes a status hierarchy where adults, especially teachers, are to be shown courtesy and respect over children.**

Here is another example that is often seen in early childhood programs:

> A preschool girl runs into the classroom excitedly, hurries past the teacher, calls happily to her friend, and runs to join the other girl at a table. The two begin to work on a puzzle together. Her grandfather, who has brought her, sternly takes her hand, pulls her back to the teacher, and demands that she greet the teacher properly. The teacher brushes off the incident by saying to the grandfather, "Oh, she's just excited to see her friend." The grandfather tells his granddaughter that she is rude. She looks down as if ashamed. The teacher pats her and says that she is too young to understand social conventions. The grandfather shakes his head sadly and leaves.

SCRIPT	NOTES

This activity can be done in a whole group or smaller groups. It is presented here as a whole-group activity.

What do you think the grandfather is thinking?

Possible answers to what the grandfather might be thinking include:

1. My granddaughter should show more respect to the teacher and to me.
2. I want my granddaughter to demonstrate good manners/have good behavior/be polite.
3. I must maintain the hierarchy of respect in my family, and my granddaughter is being rude.

What do you think the teacher is thinking?

Possible answers to what the teacher might be thinking include:

1. The child is too young to have manners.
2. I'm glad the child is eager to see her friends and work on a puzzle, an obvious learning task.
3. I'm pleased that she initiates play well.
4. That grandfather is too old-fashioned and I need to help him understand the culture of the preschool that values choices and play.

Put up **Overhead 12** again and build on the previous chart.

Individualistic Orientation	*Collectivistic Orientation*
Free to choose activities	Rules of the family
Learning activities	Social manners
Peer relations	Respect for elders

Fill in responses of the participants. In the preceding chart are some responses you might expect to hear.

NOTES

SCRIPT

Let's build on the chart we are making. Based on what we just discussed, what are the individualistic values addressed in this scenario? What are the group values?

ACTIVITY 4

Self-Reflection: Where Do You Fit?

Time: 10 minutes

Key Concepts/Experiences

- **Most people operate with some combination of individualistic and collectivistic orientations.**
- **Think about how you were raised.**
- **There is value in both.**

This is a place where the facilitator might give an example from his or her own upbringing. If there is more than one facilitator, examples can be especially enlightening, particularly if there are some differences between them. A key point to remember is that participants tend to appreciate personal stories. This is also a way of providing some informality. If possible, think of an example that is either humorous or poignant and make sure to think about what you may say ahead of time to check for its relevancy.

Most people are brought up with a combination of both sets of values: the individualistic and the collectivistic. The difference lies in which is given priority, and that differs from culture to culture.

Think for a moment about how you were brought up. Consider the degree of emphasis put on the individual, on free choice, and on the concept of personal possessions. Now consider the degree of emphasis put on the group, helping others before tending to one's own task, and sharing freely.

What examples do you have from your own experience?

SCRIPT

Talk with the person next to you, explaining how you were brought up in relation to these values. Remember this is not about being judgmental but rather about learning from each other.

NOTES

This may be a difficult disclosure for some participants, especially if they feel ambivalent about their upbringing. Reiterate the nonjudgmental aspects of the task if needed. If time permits, this is a good place to discuss how certain aspects of early childhood teacher training may be in conflict with the values with which we were raised. In the original Bridging Cultures Project, all the teachers responded individualistically at the beginning of the project, even the four Latino teachers. However, by the end of the third workshop, they had more balanced views with a clear understanding of the collectivistic perspective (see Trumbull, Diaz-Mesa, et al., 2001).

ACTIVITY 5

Thinking About Your Workplace

Time: 15 minutes

Key Concepts/Experiences

- **What is the value orientation in your workplace?**
- **Are any accommodations made for different orientations? Is there room for both?**
- **How does Developmentally Appropriate Practice relate to honoring cultural diversity?**

NOTES

Put up **Overhead 14:** Your Workplace.

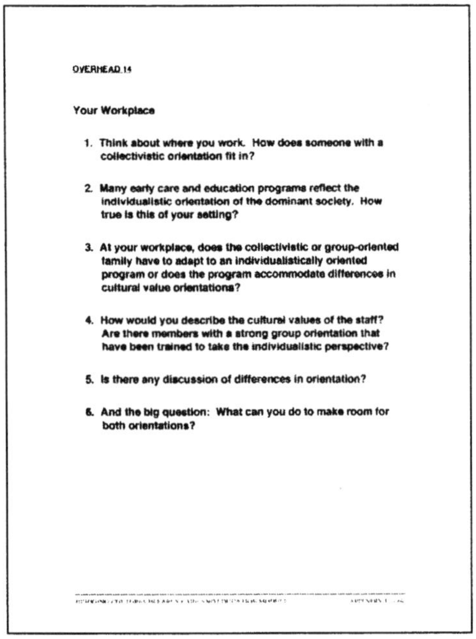
OVERHEAD 14

Your Workplace

1. Think about where you work. How does someone with a collectivistic orientation fit in?
2. Many early care and education programs reflect the individualistic orientation of the dominant society. How true is this of your setting?
3. At your workplace, does the collectivistic or group-oriented family have to adapt to an individualistically oriented program or does the program accommodate differences in cultural value orientations?
4. How would you describe the cultural values of the staff? Are there members with a strong group orientation that have been trained to take the individualistic perspective?
5. Is there any discussion of differences in orientation?
6. And the big question: What can you do to make room for both orientations?

Read this list of questions slowly, pausing between each question so participants can answer the questions in their minds. If you would like to expand this activity, you can turn this list into a checklist of *yes* or *no* and have participants think of possible examples for each. Alternatively, this might be a good place for a "quick write," providing participants with an opportunity to apply the concepts to their immediate workplace experiences. After the quick write, the facilitator can discuss some of the responses with the entire group.

"Developmentally appropriate practice" is a standard for practices and policies in early childhood programs, codified in a document of the same name by the NAEYC. Although the document challenges early childhood professionals to consider culturally appropriate practice along with child development principles,

SCRIPT

Think about where you work. How does someone with a collectivistic orientation fit in?

Many early care and education programs reflect the individualistic orientation of the dominant society. How true is this of your setting?

At your workplace, does the collectivistic or group-oriented family have to adapt to an individualistically oriented program or does the program accommodate differences in cultural value orientations?

How would you describe the cultural values of the staff? Are there members with a strong group orientation that have been trained to take the individualistic perspective?

Is there any discussion of differences in orientation?

And the big question: What can you do to make room for both orientations?

If you look at NAEYC's Developmentally Appropriate Practice, you can find a built-in mandate to respect diversity, but how that is interpreted and put into practice will vary among programs. There may be cultural tensions among staff members or with families. Understanding different cultural priorities for child growth and development and figuring out how best to address conflicts when they arise are not easy.

SCRIPT

NOTES

many people find it difficult to expand their ideas of what's appropriate beyond the examples laid out in that document. So if your participants have trouble, that's to be expected.

In this Bridging Cultures training we have asked you to suspend your judgment and accept the premise that no one value system is "correct," and that even the policies and practices of your program or agency are based on cultural values that may not comfortably fit everyone.

ACTIVITY 6 (optional—if time permits)

Proverbs

Time: 5 minutes

Key Concepts/Experiences

- **Proverbs as reflections of cultural values.**

Put up **Overhead 15:** Proverbs. (Uncover one proverb at a time.)

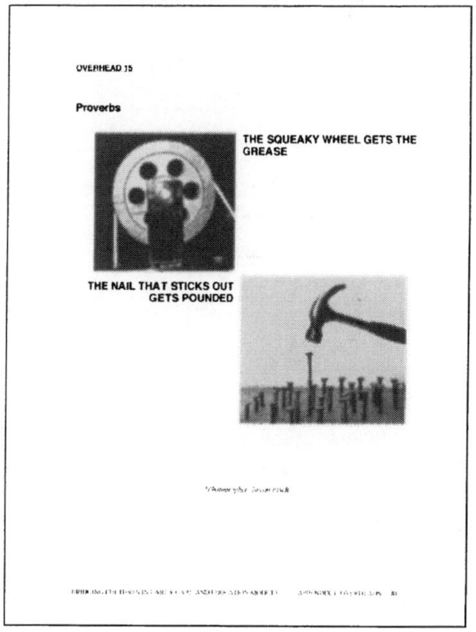

Ask participants if they can think of some other proverbs that might illustrate a focus on the individual versus a focus on the group.

NOTES | SCRIPT

Let's think about how this idea of individualism gets translated in our country. Let's look at some proverbs that stress individualism over collectivism or vice versa. What does the first one mean? What does the second one mean?

ACTIVITY 7 (optional—if time permits)

This activity is highly worthwhile and might be substituted for one of the examples, depending on the needs and interests of the participants.

Further Exploration of Patterns

Time: 15 minutes

Provide participants with **Handout 5:** Contrasting Cultural Views.

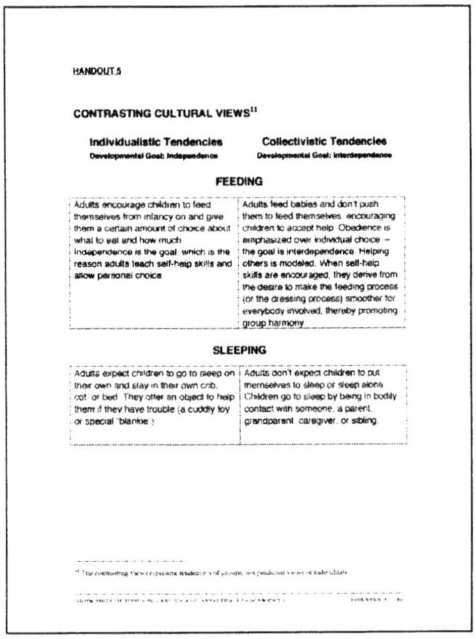

HANDOUT 5

CONTRASTING CULTURAL VIEWS[11]

Individualistic Tendencies Developmental Goal: Independence	Collectivistic Tendencies Developmental Goal: Interdependence
FEEDING	
Adults encourage children to feed themselves from infancy on and give them a certain amount of choice about what to eat and how much. Independence is the goal, which is the reason adults teach self-help skills and allow personal choice.	Adults feed babies and don't push them to feed themselves, encouraging children to accept help. Obedience is emphasized over individual choice – the goal is interdependence. Helping others is modeled. When self-help skills are encouraged, they derive from the desire to make the feeding process (or the dressing process) smoother for everybody involved, thereby promoting group harmony.
SLEEPING	
Adults expect children to go to sleep on their own and stay in their own crib, cot, or bed. They offer an object to help them if they have trouble (a cuddly toy or special "blankie").	Adults don't expect children to put themselves to sleep or sleep alone. Children go to sleep by being in bodily contact with someone, a parent, grandparent, caregiver, or sibling.

Read selected parts of the handout or allow the participants to read on their own.

Key Concepts/Experiences

- **Identify areas in the workplace where individualism and collectivism come into conflict.**

SCRIPT	NOTES
Now it's time to think about your program and how you could make a change to improve relations with the families you serve.	If appropriate, give participants the choice to work in small groups or as a whole group. The whole group would take less time and could be used to move quickly to the last part.
Take a look at the handout entitled "Contrasting Cultural Views."	For small-group activity ask the participants to organize themselves in small groups, perhaps three or four to a group. You might divide the groups into infant/toddler issues and preschool issues. Alternatively, use a method, such as numbering off, to mix up the groups for greater contact with others.
Take a few minutes to look at the comparisons, and then we are going to do one last group activity.	
To what degree do the examples here fit the conflicts you have experienced in your early childhood programs?	Take a few minutes to let people share people's ideas as a whole group.
Please share a few examples from your own experience.	

Next Steps

Learning about culture is like learning to walk. It happens one step at a time. We may fall down in the attempt, but we must persist in our efforts, knowing that the journey is worthwhile. Ultimately, the skills associated with becoming culturally competent will make our work easier because we understand the deep cultural values that motivate all kinds of behavior.

Let's make that first baby step: What is one thing you can do to be even more welcoming to each family and/or staff member in your program?

NOTES

If the participants seem lively and responsive, allow the group to share what they have learned, but watch the time. If they are exhausted, skip it.

At the very end, put up **Overhead 16:** Rumi Quotation.

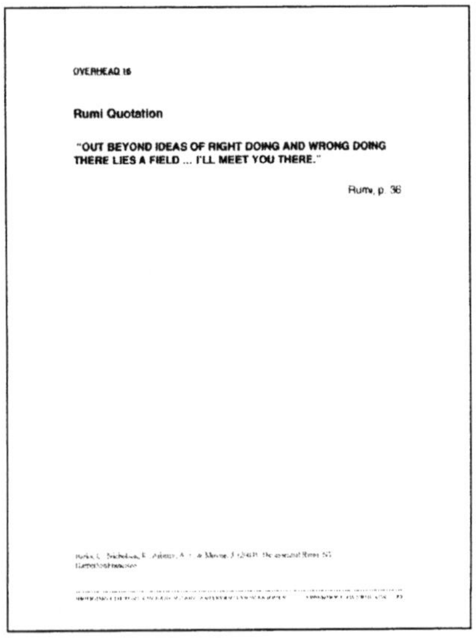
OVERHEAD 16

Rumi Quotation

"OUT BEYOND IDEAS OF RIGHT DOING AND WRONG DOING THERE LIES A FIELD ... I'LL MEET YOU THERE."

Rumi, p. 36

Recommend that participants continue to observe, discuss, respectfully ask, and read to find out more about other people's cultural value orientations.

Mention how important it is to find a setting where we are comfortable enough to examine *differences between* ourselves and others.

SCRIPT

ACTIVITY 8 (optional)

Wrap-up

Time: 10 minutes

Key Concepts/Experiences

- **Reflect on what you have learned today.**

So what did you learn today?

What can you do to continue your own learning about culture?

SCRIPT | NOTES

ACTIVITY 9

Comments About Workshop

Time: 7 minutes

Your comments about this workshop are valuable. Don't worry at all about spelling or grammar, but please do share your experiences and impressions.

Pass out **Handout 6:** Bridging Cultures in Early Care and Education: Workshop Evaluation.

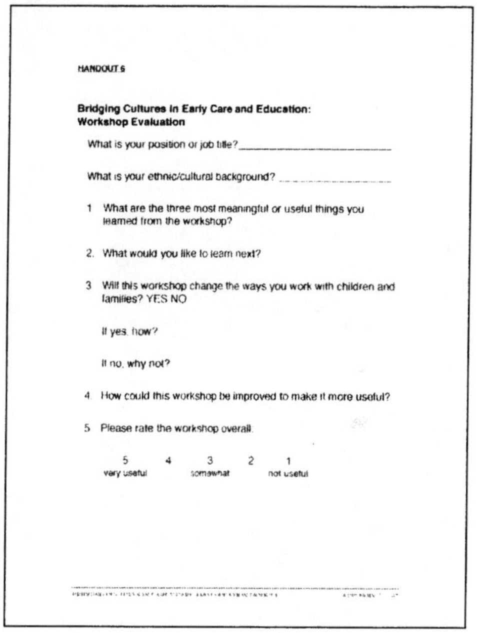
HANDOUT 6

Bridging Cultures in Early Care and Education: Workshop Evaluation

What is your position or job title? ____________

What is your ethnic/cultural background? ____________

1. What are the three most meaningful or useful things you learned from the workshop?
2. What would you like to learn next?
3. Will this workshop change the ways you work with children and families? YES NO

   If yes, how?

   If no, why not?
4. How could this workshop be improved to make it more useful?
5. Please rate the workshop overall.

   5 4 3 2 1
   very useful somewhat not useful

Take 5 minutes to complete the evaluation. I truly appreciate your participation.

After the workshop, you may want to make yourself available for questions or comments.

Chapter 3

Expanding the Learning

Photographer: Leslie Weinstock

Because a one-shot workshop rarely suffices for teaching and learning complex issues, we encourage you to expand beyond the 2-hour training presented in chapter 2. This chapter explores how the BC–ECE module can be used in different settings and for different audiences and how it can be extended beyond the script in chapter 2.

It is important to note that workshop participants will almost inevitably find themselves regarding their own workplace situations differently from the way they did before the workshop. In such instances, participants may benefit from opportunities to talk with each other about their new perceptions of what may have seemed "just the way things are" before. Participants can be encouraged to observe consciously things such as how their settings are arranged, how materials are used and shared, and how the daily schedule and duties of staff reflect particular cultural values. Staff, for example, may recognize that practices such as the use of carpet squares during circle time may encourage preschoolers to learn about personal space and it reflects individualism.[1]

Organization of the Chapter

This chapter consists of four sections. The first presents two vignette-driven activities that can be substituted for existing activities in the 2-hour workshop if the facilitator judges them to be particularly meaningful for participants. This section also suggests some independent follow-up activities for participants who wish to learn more about Bridging Cultures.

The second section proposes how to incorporate Bridging Cultures professional development or education into a range of settings. The third section is a compendium of nine activities that can be used in a longer workshop or course; each activity has been used by either the authors or close colleagues who are involved in addressing cultural issues in early childhood settings. The fourth section recommends additional resources in the broader "diversity" arena and suggests how links can be forged between BC–ECE and other diversity topics or concerns.

Section I: Revising or Expanding the Existing Workshop

Here we offer two additional activities along with suggestions for follow-up with workshop participants after they return to their own settings. Each activity can be used in conjunction with Handout 5, "Contrasting Cultural Views." One illustrates differences in approaches to play and toys, and the other highlights differences in how parents may think about toileting.

Exploring Objects

Although the following vignette was written expressly for home visitors, who may or may not work with families who have children with special needs, it may also be useful for early childhood professionals in general who sometimes face the same issue.

Vignette: Differing Ideas About Babies Exploring Objects

The home visitor sits in a small living room near a mother holding a baby. The visitor knows that the baby has some physical challenges and is at risk for developmental delays. While the mother talks to the visitor about some issues going on in her life, the visitor is wiggling a toy in front of the baby, trying to entice him to reach out for it. But the mother turns the baby around and holds him close so he can't see or reach the toy. When she hears a noise in the other room, she gets up to check on her older children. The home visitor holds out her arms to take the baby. The mother hands him to her.

The home visitor sits on the floor and holds the baby so he can easily reach any one of several toys she has arranged on a blanket. When the mother returns, the home visitor has

[1]Allowing children to sit as close to each other as they want, even virtually on top of each other, is a more collectivistic practice. In an infant/toddler program, what are the implications of highchairs lined up in a row compared with small tables and low chairs from which even babies and toddlers can crawl away on their own when they are finished? What about sleeping arrangements? Cribs with legs and high sides give one set of messages, whereas beds on the floor that are easy to crawl in and out of offer a different set of messages.

the baby lying on the blanket, and she is bent over talking to the baby, who is clutching a soft ball and waving it in the air. "Oh you like that ball! It's soft," she says. The mother picks the baby up off the blanket, and the ball falls from his hand. She ignores the ball and takes him back to her chair. As she sits down, the baby reaches for an empty plastic glass on the table beside the chair. The mother puts it out of his reach. She goes back to cuddling the baby in her arms. The home visitor looks discouraged, and the mother looks puzzled at the expression on the other woman's face.

Facilitating Discussion

Using this scene, the facilitator can ask questions, like those in the module, designed to let participants speculate why the home visitor looks discouraged and the mother looks puzzled. The point of the vignette is to get participants thinking about questions such as: What is the role of objects versus the role of social relationships in this scenario? What is the professional trying to achieve and what does she value? What is the mother trying to achieve and what does she value?

A role play in which mother and home visitor talk to each other can be a useful next step for participants. For this, participants can work in pairs or groups.

Toileting

Parent concerns about toilet training are common and can come up as an issue in infant and toddler programs. The following vignette illustrates a conflict around the timing of toilet training and serves as a basis for discussion of this issue.

Vignette: Toileting Practices in Infant and Toddler Care

A mother and a caregiver are engaged in an intense conversation. The caregiver is saying that she cannot do what the mother wants her to do, which is to put the mother's 1-year-old child on the potty at particular times of the day. The caregiver exclaims, "I just don't have time with all these other children I have to care for." In addition, the caregiver says she absolutely does not believe in toilet training a child this age. The mother tells the caregiver that her child is *already* potty trained, and all the caregiver has to do is put her child on the potty seat. The mother and caregiver are finding that they don't understand each other.

Facilitating Discussion

Using this scene, the workshop facilitator can pose questions, like those in the module, designed to let participants speculate about the feelings and thoughts of the adults in the vignette. Questions might include: What does the caregiver value? How could she better communicate to the mother? What is the mother trying to achieve, and what does she value? In addition, participants could respond to the following questions (with some input from the facilitator): What counts as being "toilet trained"? Is it when the child can independently identify when he needs to go to the potty and go by himself? Is it when he goes with a caregiver's help? What is the role of physical proximity in caregiver–child interaction in toilet training?[2] Here, too, a role play in which the mother and caregiver talk to each other can be useful for participants. Allow participants to take the role of the mother and the caregiver, either pairing off or working in groups.

---

[2]In cultures where the tendency is for mothers to hold their small children a great deal or for them otherwise to be in extreme proximity to each other, mothers can sense when a child needs to use the potty. This, understandably, is not the case when children are frequently at some distance from the caregiver.

Section II: Teaching the Training Module in Other Settings

Building on Existing Early Care and Education Professional Development on Culture

This module can be connected to specific training for infant/toddler caregivers, whether center-based staff or family child-care providers. In fact, as mentioned in the preface, the BC–ECE module is a perfect follow-up to WestEd's Program for Infant/Toddler Caregivers' (PITC) training module on culture, family, and providers (Module IV). This module addresses the relationships between caregivers and families, emphasizing the need to develop practices that are in harmony with children's home cultures. The PITC training recognizes the role of culture in a child's identity development and the need to respect families' choices of cultural identity. PITC's steps for culturally responsive caregiving could well be bywords for BC–ECE training: "*Acknowledge* differences. *Ask* for information. *Adapt* through negotiation" (Program for Infant/Toddler Caregivers, 1995, p. 135).

The training is also a good follow-up to something like the California Institute on Human Services' *Beginning Together*, a training institute designed to take PITC graduates a step further, preparing them to train staff in full-inclusion programs. Its emphasis is on collaboration between general educators and special educators in the early childhood arena, many of whom have had only limited training in cultural sensitivity. One of the strong messages for early childhood professionals is that when a child with special needs is enrolled in their program, teamwork among the teacher, family, and specialists is especially important. The kind of understanding generated by the Bridging Cultures framework can be a vital link in keeping such teams working together harmoniously.

Integrating Bridging Cultures Concepts Into College Courses

College educators can use the framework as a foundation for exploring culture within many different courses or as a module in a single course. For example, classes that focus on child growth and development could consider the framework in terms of the "ideal child"[3] and then, throughout the course, bring in examples related to individualism and collectivism. Likewise, courses on curriculum or infant and toddler care can use various scenarios to illustrate conflicts between the home and child-care settings. Courses that deal with parent involvement and education are also a natural place for discussion of individualism and collectivism. Communication is central to the relationships between parents and their children, and social conventions related to individualism and collectivism in this realm could be easily contrasted.

Convening Interdisciplinary Faculty Groups

A cross-program faculty group can be convened at the college level to explore applications to various disciplines, such as anthropology, child development, early childhood education, ethnic studies, sociology, psychology, and special education. Meetings could take the form of seminars, a format that may be comfortable and familiar for college educators.

---

[3]Participants could respond to the question: How do people from different backgrounds define the "ideal child"?

Implications for Parent Meetings or Workshops

The BC–ECE module was not designed or intended to be used directly with parents; however, much of its information could be useful to them. The module can be used to help parents understand different cultural perspectives, as well as cultural conflicts they may experience with child-care providers or teachers. Among the most important uses of the individualism–collectivism framework is making cultural values "visible" and making explicit to ourselves and others the implicit values on which we all operate. Making values explicit is especially helpful for parents from nondominant cultures who are trying to understand practices that are unfamiliar to them. One way to help parents understand the expectations of an early childhood program or early childhood services is to have parent meetings that allow exploration of potential differences between home and the early childhood setting (e.g., preschool).

Building Partnerships With Families

Too many parent meetings now focus largely on communicating information *from* professionals *to* families, conveying the notion that "we know what is best for your child and you don't." More effective are parent meetings that focus on what parents already know and build from there. In the latter approach, professionals see parental knowledge as the natural outgrowth of two things: years of experience caring for their own children and their own early childhood experiences. Parents' ideas about when and how children learn, their daily routines with their children, and the social conventions that guide parents create what Luis Moll calls "funds of knowledge" (Moll, Amanti, Neff, & Gonzalez, 1992). These aspects of parental knowledge are rooted in a family's culture. Therefore, it is helpful for professionals working with parents to view the parent–professional relationship as a partnership, where both sides have much to contribute to the development of the child.

This is a call for early care and education professionals to understand unfamiliar practices through an analysis of their own underlying value system. What would happen if parent meetings were conducted to find out more about the parents and families? What if parents and families talked about their concerns, and the professionals listened? Of course, there are times when early care professionals must explain a rule or policy that appears to conflict with what the family would do. A critical component in such conversations is an explanation of the rationale for the rule or policy. For example, state policies may prevent siblings from sleeping on the same cot. A "bridging" solution would be to allow the children to be side-by-side and perhaps share a common oversized blanket. Thus, there may be ways to adapt practices so that they work not just for the early childhood program but also for the families and children.

Helping Families With the Transition to Elementary School

Early childhood professionals have an important role in helping families understand the early childhood care and education environment, which tends to be family friendly (cf. Bredekamp & Copple, 1997). But they also have a role in helping families understand and make a smooth transition to elementary school, where the environment may be less family friendly. Parents who have had their younger children warmly welcomed at their older children's center or family child-care home may find that babies are not so welcomed in elementary school classrooms. Families need help learning about the rules, requirements, and regimens of elementary schools, which are often quite different from those of early childhood programs.

Making the cultural values of individualism clear to parents helps them understand *why* things are being done a certain way at school and what they can do at home to maintain their own cultural value system. With knowledge of both systems, they can preserve what they value in their heritage while helping their children become bicultural. For example, many teachers want children to speak up and ask questions, yet we have seen that parents with a collectivistic value orientation might find such classroom behavior rude or brazen. Professionals could explain why these skills are important in the early care and education setting while demonstrating an appreciation for the quiet respectfulness required at home by making the expectations of each setting very clear to the children. Research shows that when parents understand the rationale behind a school's expectations for the children, they will make efforts to support them (Delgado-Gaitan, 1994; Reese, 2002; Trumbull et al., 2003).

Working With Families Whose Children Have Special Needs

Understanding the differences between individualism and collectivism is especially important for those working with children with special needs. Because these professionals are charged with helping children develop to their fullest capacity, in many instances they are working to help children become more independent, as defined in a variety of ways (e.g., physically, intellectually, emotionally).

To a collectivistic parent whose orientation is to help and keep his or her child close at hand—to engender *inter*dependence rather than independence—the professional's approach may seem to conflict with the family's values. (This feeling may be intensified by the guilt that parents of children with special needs sometimes feel.) At the same time, the social worker or other professional who is not tuned into issues of collectivism and individualism may see the parent as not caring about the child's well-being.

Once the professional understands the potential for conflict, he or she can approach the situation with sensitivity and consideration. To do otherwise risks working at cross-purposes with the family. By acknowledging the legitimacy of different culture-based approaches to child development, a professional can work *with* the family and, together, they can decide on the best strategies for supporting the development of the child with special needs.

Using the Training Module at Staff Meetings

Module content can be broken up or condensed for use in situations where time is more limited, such as a faculty or staff meeting that has been set aside for discussion of cultural differences.

Study Groups

The training module can also be used as the basis for an ongoing study group for early childhood educators or other family service professionals interested in addressing diversity-related issues.

Section III: Nine Additional Activities

The exercises that follow can help create an atmosphere in which people feel comfortable sharing diverse views about culture, childrearing, childcare, and education (see also "Creating Emotional Safety" on p. 114 in Appendix D). The activities are designed to be helpful to those who are new to the concepts of the BC–ECE module as well as to those who have already explored them for some time. They have all been field tested with early childhood professionals and other family service providers. Each one deals with culture, but not strictly through the lens of individualism and collectivism. However, facilitators will find that the framework is often a useful tool for interpreting and grouping participant responses.

Some presenters will feel the need to establish an objective for each activity; others will intuitively use an activity to build on an existing objective of the workshop. Some activities can be shaped to address more than one objective. The activities are meant to be open and flexible, to be used as a means of exploration to enable participants to learn more about themselves and each other. For these reasons, we do not propose an explicit objective for each activity. As with all workshop activities, these activities may be more or less appropriate for different groups of participants.

The activities comprise: (1) You Are the Bridge, (2) Building a Continuum, (3) Your Story, (4) Give One and Get One, (5) Group Graphic: Images of Culture, (6) Brainstorming, (7) Circle-Within-a-Circle Discussion, (8) Who Are You? and (9) Leaving Home.

Activity 1. You Are the Bridge[4]

Give participants paper and felt pens. Tell them to envision a cultural bridge and think about the following: What does the bridge connect? What would the bridge look like? How long and wide would it be? What materials would be used to construct the bridge and who would build it? Then have them draw the bridge and share their drawing with another participant. If you are working with a small group, everyone can share. If it's a large group, ask for a few volunteers to share with the whole group. Another way to conduct this activity is to break up a large group into smaller groups and have each group draw one bridge. Have each group share with the larger group. This latter approach may make the activity more comfortable for the collectivistic participants.

Activity 2. Building a Continuum

Designate one end of the room as the individualistic end and the other as the collectivistic end. Ask participants to stand in a line according to where they belong on this continuum, which they find out by talking to the other people in the line. They may have to move themselves after they find out why the person next to them is standing where he or she is. Have the people on the extreme ends of the line talk to each other and explain why they placed themselves in their respective positions.

You can extend this activity further by then asking participants to arrange themselves according to how they were raised in order to see if this changes their position in the line. You can also ask them to think about themselves as early childhood educators and see if that changes their position on the line. Have a discussion about what people discovered about themselves and others from doing this exercise.

Activity 3. Your Story[5]

Ask participants to think of one experience they have had that might be explained by the framework of individualism and collectivism. Have each tell his or her story to one other person, describing what happened and how cultural values might have been at play. Ask participants to give as much detail as possible. Ask for volunteers to

---

[4]Adapted from Rothstein-Fisch, 2003a, with permission of copyright holder.
[5]Adapted from Rothstein-Fisch, 2003a, with permission of copyright holder.

share their story with the whole group. An alternative way to carry out this activity is to ask participants to write their stories and then share them either with the whole group, a small group, or another individual.

Keep in mind that for collectivistically oriented students, being asked to share with the whole group may make them feel like "the nail that sticks out," so using smaller groups for discussion may be more effective in getting people to share freely.

Activity 4. Give One and Get One[6]

Have each participant write his or her name at the top of a piece of paper and then fold the paper in half the long way. Then have them open it up and number 1 to 12 down the left side and, again, down the fold, thereby creating a left-hand column and a right-hand column. Explain that the purpose of this activity is to share ideas about two topics. Have participants label the left-hand column as "Adult behaviors that indicate more of a collectivistic orientation" and the right-hand column as "Adult behaviors that indicate more of an individualistic orientation."

Ask participants to write something by number 1 in each column, then walk around and share with each other what they have written. In doing so, they are to collect ideas about what to write under the other numbers. When writing down someone else's idea, they should also record the name of the person who originated the idea. To facilitate the reporting, ask for one person to share an idea that he or she got from someone else and to name that person. That person then shares an idea that he or she got from someone else. This way no one takes credit for his or her own ideas but rather puts the spotlight on someone else, which makes this a more collectivistic way of conducting an activity. This approach gives participants a chance to learn from each other in an active-learning format. Discussion afterward can focus on the differences in perspective. It's important to respect diversity in this exercise. It isn't about right and wrong but about perspectives. A variation for this exercise is to identify *child* behaviors rather than adult behaviors.

Activity 5. Group Graphic: Images of Culture[7]

Divide participants into groups of about six people. Ask the question: "What is culture?" Have poster paper and felt pens available for each group to answer the question using only images and symbols, no words. Moving away from the verbal mode opens the way for participants who are usually quiet to become more engaged. Let each group explain its graphic. If participants are already well grounded in the framework of individualism and collectivism, have a class discussion about whether any of the images they use reflect concepts captured by the framework.

If the participants aren't well grounded in the framework, you can do the activity anyway, but after they have done the first step, put the graphics aside and do some further training on the framework. Afterward, bring out the graphics again and ask participants if they want to add any more images or modify existing images. In a college class, this exercise can be used twice, as an informal pre- and post-test to see how much participants have learned about the framework and how it might have influenced their thinking about culture.

---

[6]Thanks to Intisar Shareef for this activity.

[7]Thanks to Intisar Shareef for this activity.

Activity 6. Brainstorming

Write the word *Collectivism* or *Individualism* on a board or chart paper. Ask participants what comes to mind when they hear or see that word. Explain that you're doing a brainstorming exercise to explore various associations that come up for people. The idea is for them to say the first thing that comes to mind. Write down the words and phrases they come up with. If they are coming fast, get two people to write. Don't censor, correct, question, or comment. Write down whatever participants say. Don't laugh or allow participants to laugh. A facilitator's comments or facial expressions of surprise or puzzlement can dampen participants' creativity, so be neutral and accepting. It can, however, be helpful to ask contributors to say why they associate certain words or images with either individualism or collectivism. A facilitator might simply ask, "Do you want to say more about that?"

Examples offered by participants often revolve around relationships that may not be part of early care and learning experiences. For example, someone might say, "Barbeque—because my boyfriend makes us spend all our weekends with his family," or "Placemats—because they define individual space on the table, and it makes me feel uncomfortable that I have to eat in a confined way." Keep the exercise going for a while, even if it begins to slow down. Push past the natural stopping place to help participants think more broadly, deeply, and creatively. When words stop coming, ask them to think of images and have them turn the images into words.

When you feel you have reached the end, ask participants to choose one of the following tasks, using the words that you've recorded: (a) write a definition; (b) create a poem; (c) make up a song; (d) create an image or symbol; (e) draw a picture; (f) make up a dance, movement, gesture, machine, human sculpture, or some other body expression; (g) create a role play. Letting participants choose from a wide variety of expressive forms allows greater involvement by those who might otherwise hang back.

Participants can work individually or in small groups. Have participants in each group share what they came up with. It's important not to analyze or critique the products. A final discussion question could be, "What did you learn from this activity?" If the training is going to be more than a single session, this exercise can also be used as a pre- or post-test. At the end of the training, participants can do the exercise again and see how different the responses are from the first time they did it. If the activity is used this way, the products of the first exercise should be saved so they can be compared with the products of the second exercise. One of the advantages of this exercise is that if participants are given a choice of mode of expression, they may be freed from the common tendency to operate in a more academic, literary, or linear mode.

Activity 7. Circle-Within-a-Circle Discussion

This activity works best if you have a diverse audience, but even if the group doesn't look diverse, you may be surprised to discover the range of collectivistic and individualistic orientations that are represented.

Arrange chairs so that there are inner and outer circles. Ask participants who see themselves as more collectivistic if they would be willing to sit in the inner circle and discuss their perspective on common early childhood practices, or even uncommon practices, that they have experienced. Alternatively, they could just talk about what it means to be more collectivistic, how it feels, and what their experiences are when they are around more individualistic people or in individualistic settings.

Another approach is to ask people how their upbringing made them more collectivistic than individualistic. The people in the inner circle discuss the topic while the people in the outer circle observe. After a designated time, the people in the outer circle discuss what they observed. Then, collectivists leave the inner circle, and the individualists are invited to take their places and discuss the same or similar questions while the others observe. This is a good way to organize the number of people in a large group and still involve everyone. It also lets the group observe and comment on the discussion. An alternative way to conduct this exercise is to start with the individualists in the inner circle.

Activity 8. Who Are You?

Have participants take out a piece of paper and number it vertically from 1 to 15 down the left-hand side. Then match each participant with a partner he or she does not know very well and ask the teams to choose which partner will write first. The activity requires the writer to ask his or her partner the same question—"Who are you?"—15 times and to record each response next to the appropriate number. Tell the partners who are responding to the question that they should give a different answer each time and that their answers should be quick, short, and off the top of the head.

When the question has been asked and answered 15 times, with all the answers recorded, the partners switch roles, with the responder becoming the questioner. Each pair then analyzes both sets of responses, looking for patterns or sorting them into categories such as roles, relationships, or personal qualities, attributes, or interests. They can make up their own categories. When they have finished, ask each team to discuss how many of each person's answers relate to individualistic views of self and how many relate to collectivistic views of self. If they don't see a connection, suggest that listing personal qualities or traits, such as "I am artistic" or "I am a good athlete," may reflect a more individualistic view. Answering in terms of roles, relationships, and group affiliations, such as "I'm a mother," "teacher," "wife," or "Muslim," may reflect a more collectivistic view. See if they agree.

As a group, discuss what participants got out of the exercise. Do any patterns occur that are particularly interesting? When adequate trust has been built, this activity can be used with a beginning, intermediate, or advanced group. It's a good way to help people get to know each other better.

Activity 9. Leaving Home

What does the term "leave home" mean to you? In your family, do the children grow up and leave home? Did you or will you leave home? Did your parents leave home? Do you have a story to tell about leaving home or not leaving home?

This activity, conducted as a "go-round" or a "round robin," involves posing a question or set of questions to stimulate participants to share their own experiences. It works well to use some kind of talking stick or other object for participants to pass around to mark the change of turns; the person talking can choose how long to go on and when to pass the stick to the next person. If there are time constraints, make it clear how long each person may talk. If it seems helpful, you can, instead, appoint a timekeeper. Either way, be sure to get all the way around the group before the time is up so that every participant has a chance to share. Allow participants to pass if they choose, but leave time at the end, so those who passed once can then share if they have changed their mind.

This activity could be useful for getting diverse perspectives on any topic. Discussing a topic that is familiar to everyone can reveal cultural patterns and, therefore, can serve as cultural research. It also helps participants get to know each other and appreciate differences. The activity only works if judgment is suspended and the facilitator makes it clear that there are no right or wrong answers because everything is based on personal experience. Participants should be asked whether they can discern any patterns related to individualism or collectivism related to their own experience.

This isn't designed to categorize people, only to explore diversity in experiences. Therefore, people should be warned not to generalize or to interpret others' experiences. Facilitators should take special care to ensure that no one seeks to invalidate someone else's experience. The point is that each person speaks his or her own truth, though it isn't the same as someone else's truth.

Caution: Don't let the go-round turn into a discussion before everyone has had a chance to speak.

Leaving home is a good topic for anyone who has had to make a difficult or painful decision to move away from his or her family, for whatever reason, including pursuing higher education. If people speak about problems or conflicts (and they have at our pilot testing and in our work), see if the participant can describe how the problem was resolved, but don't interrupt the go-round by focusing on problem solving a person's situation if it hasn't been resolved.

This activity can now lead to a discussion about separation in young children and how adult experiences with and feelings about separation can be used to understand young children's feelings and behaviors. Most early childhood educators, as well as other professionals, find that the issue of separation is powerful and interesting to people. Some special educators find the issue looms even larger when parents of children with disabilities have to leave their children for the first time without having full confidence and trust in the person to whom they are entrusting their child. It's easy to call those parents "overprotective" without understanding their unique situation.[8] The more diverse and sophisticated the group, the deeper the discussion can go into cultural differences, but even with beginners the discussion can become intensely interesting. Even in a seemingly monocultural group, there are enormous differences in experiences around this issue.

A follow-up for this activity is to ask how each person's experience of leaving home related or didn't relate to family patterns. Did others leave? What was expected of adult children? Have them think about their parents' stories (if they know them) and their grandparents' stories. A good deal of cultural information can come out when exploring the attitudes and practices of previous generations.

Section IV: Connecting to Other Diversity Education

This section addresses different aspects of diversity that others have addressed successfully and with which BC–ECE professional development should, ideally, be linked. Complete reference information for each publication or product mentioned is included in the References at the end of the module.

It is important to recognize that just as a culture continues to change over time, so do the theories that attempt to describe it. Therefore, staying current in the field is important, whether through

[8]It may not be possible to discern how the framework fits or doesn't fit the various experiences people share. But the focus should be brought back to what the framework can explain.

membership in organizations that publish regularly on the topic or by looking for new resources on the Internet and, of course, through colleagues. Staying abreast of new professional development opportunities for professionals working with children from birth to age 5 will assist you.

Antibias/Antiracist Professional Development

Many participants in the module's pilot sessions mentioned that they had either taken or given antibias workshops based on the work of Louise Derman-Sparks and the Antibias Task Force (1989). *Teaching/Learning Anti-Racism: A Developmental Approach* (Derman-Sparks & Phillips, 1997) is also an excellent resource. While the BC–ECE module addresses culture, the antibias and antiracist literature and professional development deal with inequalities in power between the races in the United States and their consequences. Both cultural and racial differences can lead to what has been called "the power differential," resulting in serious inequities for children and families. Another excellent resource that deals broadly with power issues and with the notion of "cultural proficiency"[9] is *Cultural Proficiency: A Manual for School Leaders* (Lindsey, Nuri Robins, & Terrell, 2003). This book is ideal for teacher educators or experienced professional developers.

Comprehensive Diversity Training

The BC–ECE module can be incorporated into a comprehensive training program, such as the Southwest Educational Development Laboratory's (SEDL) *Understanding the Cultural Contexts of Teaching and Learning* (Guerra & Garcia, 2000). SEDL's training program includes a Bridging Cultures workshop as one of 11 day-long (or longer) training sessions. The other sessions address such cultural dimensions as power–distance and low- and high-context communication styles, field dependence, and field independence. Understanding of some of these other constructs is enhanced by knowledge of the individualism–collectivism framework.

Another worthwhile resource is *Developing Cross-Cultural Competence: A Guide for Working with Children and Their Families* (Lynch & Hanson, 1998), which offers chapters specific to different cultural groups, such as Native American, Asian, Latino, African American, Middle Eastern, Native Hawaiian and Samoan, Pilipino, and Anglo-European.

Also worth exploring is BANDTEC (A Network for Diversity Training, Building Equity and Social Justice for Children and Families), an organization committed to the understanding of diversity in early care and education communities. One of its publications, *Reaching for Answers: A Workbook on Diversity in Early Childhood Education* (2003), contains a number of activities and resources relevant to diversity training that could be used to expand BC–ECE training. BANDTEC can be contacted through its Web site: www.bandtec.org.

Intercultural Communication

Several worthwhile resources have helped shape our thinking, and we pass these along to encourage an ever-widening interest in cross-cultural understanding. The first two are particularly salient for professionals working with special needs populations, and the last set of resources is more general

[9] Also referred to as *cultural competence, cultural proficiency* is used broadly to refer to skill in understanding, accepting, and responding constructively to differences based on race, culture, gender, gender identity, age, class, and religion.

in focus. *Skilled Dialogue* (Barrera, with Corso & Macpherson, 2003) discusses many aspects of diversity as well as assessment and intervention in early childhood settings. The authors present many useful ways to think about communication and provide specific techniques for facilitating conversation across cultural boundaries. Another helpful book that explores cross-cultural competence with special needs populations is *Interactions: Collaboration Skills for School Professionals* (Friend & Cook, 2003), which includes material related to Bridging Cultures content and describes methods of interpersonal communication, problem solving, and putting ideas into practice.

A more general book on intercultural communication is *Intercultural Competence: Interpersonal Communication, 4th ed.* (Lustig & Koester, 2003), which is most useful, we think, for learning about cross-cultural communication. The book is designed as a text, with many wonderful examples of applying theories of cultural communication to daily life. Discussions of ethical and social issues are also included.

All three of these books offer skill-building sessions on communication. Two interesting resources on cross-cultural communication in a variety of settings are *Intercultural Interactions: A Practical Guide* (Cushner & Brislin, 1996) and *Intercultural Communication in the Global Workplace* (Varner & Beamer, 2004). Another book that is not aimed at a cross-cultural audience but is an excellent resource on improving communication skills is *Crucial Conversations* (Patterson, Grenny, McMillan, & Switzler, 2002).

Attachment and Separation

If a training focuses at all on attachment, a helpful resource for the facilitator and participants is *Culture and Attachment: Perceptions of the Child in Context* (Harwood, Miller, & Irizarry, 1995). This book would be useful as background to Activity 9, "Leaving Home," and could give facilitators ideas for how to expand on that activity.

Looking Back and Moving Forward

In this chapter, we present ideas for extending the learning initiated by the training described in chapter 2 and adapting it to different contexts. We believe facilitators will find it easy to adapt the 2-hour training to the needs of a variety of audiences—from preschool teachers to family daycare providers, kindergarten teachers, and health care professionals. Of course, we encourage module users to alter the sequence and form of activities to suit their participants.

Appendix A

Workshop Overheads

Overhead 1: Professional Development Objectives

Overhead 2: Module Agenda

Overhead 3: Baby in High Chair

Overhead 4: Mother Spoon-Feeding Her Preschooler

Overhead 5: All About Me

Overhead 6: Chart of Individual and Group Orientation

Overhead 7: Greenfield Quotation

Overhead 8: Hofstede's Individualism Ratings

Overhead 9: Beware of Overgeneralizing

Overhead 10: Culture Is Invisible

Overhead 11: Playing With Blocks

Overhead 12: Blank Chart of Individualism and Collectivism

Overhead 13: First Thing in the Morning

Overhead 14: Your Workplace

Overhead 15: Proverbs

Overhead 16: Rumi Quotation

Professional Development Objectives

- **Recognize contrasting cultural patterns in the care and education of young children**
- **Reflect on personal values and values implicit in program practices**
- **Expand definitions of culturally responsive care and education**
- **Consider new ways to promote equity in early childhood care and education**

Zepeda, M., Gonzalez-Mena, J., Rothstein-Fisch, C., & Trumbull, E. (2006). *Bridging Cultures in Early Care and Education: A Training Module* (p. 61). Copyright 2006. Mahwah, NJ: Lawrence Erlbaum Associates.

OVERHEAD 2

Module Agenda

- **Contrasting Approaches**

  Activity 1: Contrasting approaches to feeding

- **Building a Framework: Individualism and collectivism**

  Activity 2: Thinking in terms of patterns: Individual orientation and group orientation

  Activity 3: Exploring patterns in practice

  Activity 4: Self-reflection: Where do you fit?

  Activity 5: Thinking about your workplace

  Activity 6: Proverbs (optional)

  Activity 7: Further exploration of patterns (optional)

- **Reflection**

  Activity 8: Wrap-up (optional)

- **Evaluation**

  Activity 9: Comments about workshop

OVERHEAD 3

Baby in High Chair

Video Still from Magna Systems, copyright 1996, Magna Systems

OVERHEAD 4

Mother Spoon-Feeding Her Preschooler

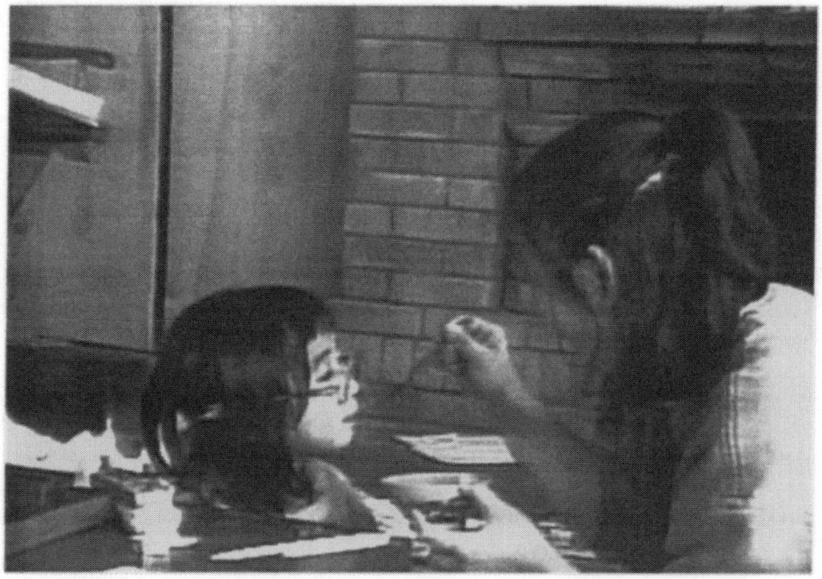

Video Still from Magna Systems, copyright 1996, Magna Systems

OVERHEAD 5

All About Me

Photographer: Marlene Zepeda

OVERHEAD 6

Chart of Individual and Group Orientation

Individual Orientation	*Group Orientation*
Focus on individual development and functioning independently by • Helping oneself • Having a right to one's property	Focus on interdependence and the child as a member of a group • Helping others • Sharing property

Zepeda, M., Gonzalez-Mena, J., Rothstein-Fisch, C., & Trumbull, E. (2006). *Bridging Cultures in Early Care and Education: A Training Module* (p. 71). Copyright 2006. Mahwah, NJ: Lawrence Erlbaum Associates.

OVERHEAD 7

Greenfield Quotation

Psychology as the science of the individual was born and nourished by the philosophical foundations of individualism. We now discover that the independent individual is not a universal fact, but a culture-specific belief system about the development of a person. There is an important alternative belief system that is held by about 70% of the world's population (Triandis, 1989); it is called interdependence or collectivism.

Greenfield, P. M. (1994). Independence and interdependence as developmental scripts: Implications for theory, research, and practice. In P. M. Greenfield & R. R. Cocking (Eds.), *Cross-cultural roots of minority child development* (pp. 1–37). Hillsdale, NJ: Lawrence Erlbaum Associates, p. 3.

OVERHEAD 8

Hofstede's Individualism Ratings

USA	91
Australia	90
Great Britain	89
Canada	80
Italy	76
France, Sweden	71
Germany	67
Israel	54
Spain	51
India	48
Argentina, Japan	47
Iran	41
"Arab countries," Brazil	38
Philippines	32
Mexico	30
Hong Kong	25
Singapore, Thailand	20
"West African countries"	20
South Korea	18
Costa Rica	15
Indonesia, Pakistan	14
Guatemala	6

OVERHEAD 9

Beware of Overgeneralizing

Photographer: Bryan Fisch

- **No one culture—or person—is either individualistic or collectivistic. Personal histories are important in shaping these differences.**
- **Some people have strong aspects of both value orientations and some consider themselves bicultural.**
- **But to ignore culture is to hobble development, the role of the family, and the role of early childhood professionals.**

OVERHEAD 10

Culture Is Invisible

Culture is like the water fish swim in—a reality that is taken for granted, rarely examined.

Photographer: Christian Holden

Varner, I., & Beamer, L. (2004). *Intercultural communication in the global workplace* (3rd ed.). New York: McGraw-Hill, p. 5.

Zepeda, M., Gonzalez-Mena, J., Rothstein-Fisch, C., & Trumbull, E. (2006). *Bridging Cultures in Early Care and Education: A Training Module* (p. 79). Copyright 2006. Mahwah, NJ: Lawrence Erlbaum Associates.

OVERHEAD 11

Playing With Blocks

Photographer: Carrie Rothstein-Fisch

Zepeda, M., Gonzalez-Mena, J., Rothstein-Fisch, C., & Trumbull, E. (2006). *Bridging Cultures in Early Care and Education: A Training Module* (p. 81). Copyright 2006. Mahwah, NJ: Lawrence Erlbaum Associates.

OVERHEAD 12

Blank Chart of Individualism and Collectivism

Individualistic Orientation	*Collectivistic Orientation*

Zepeda, M., Gonzalez-Mena, J., Rothstein-Fisch, C., & Trumbull, E. (2006). *Bridging Cultures in Early Care and Education: A Training Module* (p. 83). Copyright 2006. Mahwah, NJ: Lawrence Erlbaum Associates.

OVERHEAD 13

First Thing in the Morning

Photographer: Carrie Rothstein-Fisch

OVERHEAD 14

Your Workplace

1. Think about where you work. How does someone with a collectivistic orientation fit in?
2. Many early care and education programs reflect the individualistic orientation of the dominant society. How true is this of your setting?
3. At your workplace, does the collectivistic or group-oriented family have to adapt to an individualistically oriented program, or does the program accommodate differences in cultural value orientations?
4. How would you describe the cultural values of the staff? Are there members with a strong group orientation that have been trained to take the individualistic perspective?
5. Is there any discussion of differences in orientation?
6. And the big question: What can you do to make room for both orientations?

OVERHEAD 15

Proverbs

THE SQUEAKY WHEEL GETS THE GREASE

THE NAIL THAT STICKS OUT GETS POUNDED

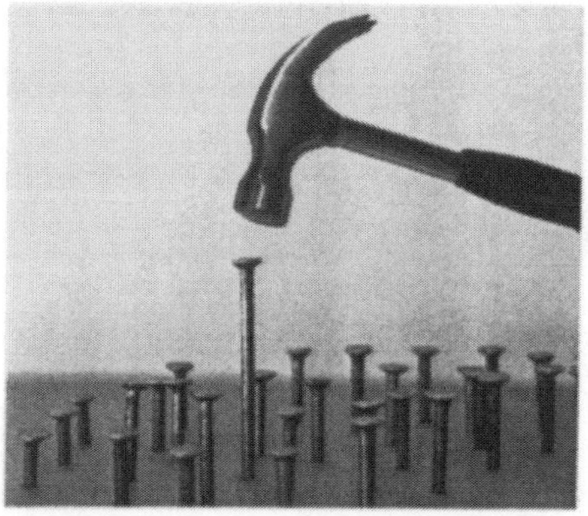

Photographer: Bryan Fisch

OVERHEAD 16

Rumi Quotation

OUT BEYOND IDEAS OF RIGHT DOING AND WRONG DOING THERE LIES A FIELD . . . I'LL MEET YOU THERE.

—Rumi, as quoted in Barks, Nicholson, Arberry, and Moyne, 2004, p. 36

Barks, C., Nicholson, R., Arberry, A. J., & Moyne, J. (2004). *The essential Rumi.* San Francisco: Harper.

Appendix B

Workshop Handouts

Handout 1: How Two Mothers Feed Their Children

Handout 2: All About Me

Handout 3: Playing With Blocks

Handout 4: First Thing in the Morning

Handout 5: Contrasting Cultural Views

Handout 6: Bridging Cultures in Early Care and Education: Workshop Evaluation

HANDOUT 1

How Two Mothers Feed Their Children

1. What might the first mother say about why she thinks she is doing a *good* job in how she feeds her child?

2. What might the second mother say about why she thinks she is doing a *good* job in how she feeds her child?

3. What might the first mother say about the way the second mother is feeding her child?

4. What might the second mother say about the way the first mother is feeding her child?

HANDOUT 2

All About Me

Each child in the preschool group is making a book called *All About Me*. The teacher asks each one to say what is special about himself or herself. The teacher writes the child's comment and the child draws a picture to go with the words. One boy responds to the question with examples about other people: His brother is very good at soccer, and his father is very good at cooking. The teacher keeps asking the boy to describe qualities about *himself*, prompting him by saying: "This is all about YOU. Are you smart? Yes, of course you are smart, so let's say you are special because you are smart." In the end, the boy's book contained drawings with dictated sentences such as "I am special because I am strong, and I am special because I am smart, and I am special because I am handsome." When the boy's mother sees the book she looks distressed instead of delighted, as the teacher had expected.

1. Why does the teacher think this is a good activity?

2. What is the child thinking?

3. What is the parent thinking?

4. What is the teacher thinking about the mother's reaction?

Zepeda, M., Gonzalez-Mena, J., Rothstein-Fisch, C., & Trumbull, E. (2006). *Bridging Cultures in Early Care and Education: A Training Module* (p. 97). Copyright 2006. Mahwah, NJ: Lawrence Erlbaum Associates.

HANDOUT 3

Playing With Blocks

At preschool, a girl is playing with blocks. A boy who is playing nearby takes one of the blocks that the girl is not using. The girl protests saying, "That's mine!" The teacher comes over and says to the boy, "Now, she used her words to tell you that's her block. You need to listen to her and ask permission if you want to use it." The boy's mother is in another part of the room, and a look of shock is on her face at the way the teacher handled the incident.

In a small group of three to four people, spend 10 minutes discussing what is happening here.

1. What might the boy be thinking or feeling? What cultural value orientation—individualism or collectivism—motivates his behavior?

2. What might the girl be thinking or feeling? What is her cultural value orientation?

3. What values does the teacher seem to hold? What things seem most important to her?

4. What is the boy's mother thinking or feeling? What might her values be?

HANDOUT 4

First Thing in the Morning

A preschool girl runs into the classroom excitedly, hurries past the teacher, calls happily at her friend and runs to join the other girl at a table. The two begin to work on a puzzle together. Her grandfather, who has brought her, sternly takes her hand, pulls her back to the teacher, and demands that she greet the teacher properly. The teacher brushes off the incident by saying to the grandfather, "Oh, she's just excited to see her friend." The grandfather tells his granddaughter that she is rude. She looks down as if ashamed. The teacher pats her and says that she is too young to understand social conventions. The grandfather shakes his head sadly and leaves.

1. What do you think the grandfather is thinking?

2. What do you think the teacher is thinking?

Zepeda, M., Gonzalez-Mena, J., Rothstein-Fisch, C., & Trumbull, E. (2006). *Bridging Cultures in Early Care and Education: A Training Module* (p. 101). Copyright 2006. Mahwah, NJ: Lawrence Erlbaum Associates.

HANDOUT 5

Contrasting Cultural Views[1]

Individualistic Tendencies Developmental Goal: Independence	Collectivistic Tendencies Developmental Goal: Interdependence

FEEDING

Adults encourage children to feed themselves from infancy on and give them a certain amount of choice about what to eat and how much. Independence is the goal, which is the reason adults teach self-help skills and allow personal choice.	Adults feed babies and don't push them to feed themselves, encouraging children to accept help. Obedience is emphasized over individual choice—the goal is interdependence. Helping others is modeled. When self-help skills are encouraged, they derive from the desire to make the feeding process (or the dressing process) smoother for everybody involved, thereby promoting group harmony.

SLEEPING

Adults expect children to go to sleep on their own and stay in their own crib, cot, or bed. They offer an object to help them if they have trouble (a cuddly toy or special "blankie").	Adults don't expect children to put themselves to sleep or sleep alone. Children go to sleep by being in bodily contact with someone, a parent, grandparent, caregiver, or sibling.

[1]The contrasting views represent tendencies of groups, not predicted views of individuals.

TOILETING

Toilet *learning* starts when the child shows signs of physical, intellectual, and emotional readiness by indicating he or she needs to use the potty, getting to the potty without help, pulling down pants, etc. The goal is independence and self-care in toileting.	Toilet *training* requires the adult to anticipate when the child needs to use the potty. The child's body can become conditioned to use the potty during the first year of life with the help of an empathetic and patient adult. Close physical proximity and a sensitivity to the baby helps adults know when to take the infant to the toilet.

SEPARATION

Although adults may experience difficulty in separating, they expect that children can learn to separate at an early age and that new attachments to caregivers can readily occur.	Adults have difficulty separating and they don't perceive the ability to separate early in life as an important developmental goal. Care outside of the extended family may be emotionally difficult for the parents and the child.

LEARNING AND PLAY

Learning is child centered and involves play, exploration, and individual choice.	Learning is adult directed and depends more on observation than play, exploration, and child choice.
Playing with objects and materials is a good way to learn about the physical world as well as about personal possessions. Children must first choose whether to understand themselves as possessors of objects before they can learn to share them. They are often allowed to share.	Objects are less important than relationships. Objects used in play are seen as a means of helping social interactions or teaching children to share. Sharing is stressed from the beginning of life and little emphasis is placed on personal ownership. Sharing is not a choice.
Play is enjoyed between adults and children.	Play most often occurs among siblings, cousins, or other children.

LANGUAGE AND COMMUNICATION

Language development is emphasized through encouraging verbal skills. Adults initiate conversation with children and ask questions. They describe what children do and elaborate on what children say.	Much communication is nonverbal. Unspoken communication is valued and children learn language through observation and modeling, by being on the edge of adult conversations but not entering them, and from siblings.
Adults model honest and direct communication and encourage children's self-expression. Adults acknowledge children's feelings and give them words to express them.	Adults model indirect communication because it leaves room for "face saving." They teach children that respect for elders is more important than individual self-expression. Social harmony is more important than expression of individual feelings.

HANDOUT 6

Bridging Cultures in Early Care and Education: Workshop Evaluation

What is your position or job title? ______________________________

What is your ethnic/cultural background? ______________________________

1. What are the three most meaningful or useful things you learned from the workshop?

2. What would you like to learn next?

3. Will this workshop change the ways you work with children and families? YES NO
   If yes, how?

   If no, why not?

4. How could this workshop be improved to make it more useful?

5. Please rate the workshop overall:

5	4	3	2	1
very useful		somewhat		not useful

Appendix C

Hofstede's Ratings of 50 Countries and Three Regions[1]

The Index of Individualism shows how each country or region was rated on a scale from 0 (*least individualistic*) to 100 (*most individualistic*). The countries are listed alphabetically.

Index of Individualism

Argentina 46
Australia 90
Austria 55
Belgium 75
Brazil 38
Canada 80
Chile 23
Colombia 13
Costa Rica 15
Denmark 74
Ecuador 8
Finland 63
France 71
Germany 67
Great Britain 89
Greece 35
Guatemala 6
Hong Kong 25
Indonesia 14
India 48
Iran 41
Ireland 70
Israel 54
Italy 76
Jamaica 39
Japan 46
Korea (South) 18
Malaysia 26
Mexico 30
Netherlands 80
Norway 69
New Zealand 79
Pakistan 14
Panama 11
Peru 16
Philippines 32
Portugal 27
South Africa 65
Salvador 19
Singapore 20
Spain 51
Sweden 71
Switzerland 68
Taiwan 17
Thailand 20
Turkey 37
Uruguay 36
United States 91
Venezuela 12
Yugoslavia 27

---

[1]The index is from *Culture's Consequences: Comparing Values, Behaviors, Institutions, and Organizations Across Nations* (2nd ed.) (p. 215), by G. Hofstede, 2001, Thousand Oaks, CA: Sage. Copyright 2001 by Geert Hofstede. Adapted with permission.

In the original study the data from certain countries were aggregated and the countries grouped as a region: East Africa (Ethiopia, Kenya, Tanzania, Zambia) 27; West Africa (Ghana, Nigeria, Sierra Leone) 20; Arab countries (Egypt, Iraq, Kuwait, Lebanon, Libya, Saudi Arabia, United Arab Emirates) 38.

Hofstede's work across 72 countries focused on local IBM employees. Although the objective was to study the work patterns and work-related goals of the employees, the analysis revealed that the various countries in which they worked could be characterized by their relative cultural differences. Hofstede found that the individualism and collectivism framework has implications for many social sciences, including education, about which he writes:

> The purpose of education is perceived differently by individualist and collectivist societies. In the former, education is seen as aimed at preparing the individual for a place in society of other individuals. This means learning to cope with new, unknown, unforeseen situations . . . the purpose of learning is not so much to know *how to do* as it is *how to learn*. . . . In the collectivist society, education stresses adaptation to the skills and virtues necessary to be an acceptable group member. This leads to a premium of the products of tradition. Learning is more often seen as a one-time process, reserved for the young only, who have to learn *how to do things* in order to participate in society. (Hofstede, 2001, p. 235)

Appendix D

Best Use of the Training Module[1]

This appendix is intended to help prepare new BC–ECE presenters. It describes specific background reading to help anchor presenters' understanding of the theoretical framework of individualism and collectivism. It also makes suggestions for how to deal with a few important issues that commonly arise in discussions about culture. Finally, for those new not just to BC–ECE but also to presentation in general, this section offers some more-generic guidance. But first, a couple of caveats:

Because it is impossible to know everything about any culture, even one's own, presenters should not be inhibited by a concern that they "don't know enough." Gaining knowledge and insight about different cultures and the role of culture in human behavior is a continuous process that requires an open mind and an open heart. Such knowledge can be acquired in part by reading. But observing people and asking questions in a respectful, nonjudgmental way is another important route to learning about other cultures. By modeling and encouraging participants to take this approach, facilitators can enable all involved to learn from each other during the workshop.

Also, the BC–ECE process can be challenging for presenters and participants alike. It is often said that to understand another person's culture we must understand our own. Therefore, self-awareness is the first step in making a connection to others. What makes us the same? What makes us different? There are no easy answers to these fundamental questions. In pursuing answers, we must be prepared to accept ambiguity and to try to accept—or at least understand—points of view that differ from our own and with which we might disagree.

---

[1]The content of this appendix is drawn largely from the *Bridging Cultures Teacher Education Module* by C. Rothstein-Fisch, 2003, Mahwah, NJ: Lawrence Erlbaum Associates. Copyright 2003 by Lawrence Erlbaum Associates. Used with permission. The suggestions have proved useful for the training of elementary school personnel and are added here for presenters who may want to review or refresh their presentation skills.

Building Background for the Workshop

Reading widely about culture, race, language, and power relations is helpful in preparing to facilitate a workshop. As mentioned earlier, the Bridging Cultures Project has several publications that can inform and support the use of this early childhood module. To begin, we highly recommend *Readings for Bridging Cultures: Teacher Education Module* (Rothstein-Fisch, 2003b). This collection of articles provides presenters with additional examples of how the individualism–collectivism framework can be applied. Also, in Appendix F of this module, we provide an annotated bibliography highlighting relevant theory in child and cross-cultural psychology that users may find helpful for understanding the role of culture in child growth and development.

As a way to gain a greater understanding of the Bridging Cultures Project and its impact on home–school relations, we also recommend *Bridging Cultures: Teacher Education Module* (Rothstein-Fisch, 2003a) and *Bridging Cultures Between Home and School: A Guide for Teachers* (Trumbull, Greenfield, et al., 2001).

Making the Time Commitment

Before their first workshop, facilitators are strongly encouraged to read about diversity in the publications listed in the bibliography and, in particular, those developed by the Bridging Cultures Project. Facilitators can develop their understanding of cultural differences by considering how the various concepts presented in their reading relate to their own personal and professional experiences. This type of reflection should be encouraged and modeled in the workshop, and participants must be given sufficient time to consider, absorb, and relate what they are learning to their own histories and work with children and families. Important learning takes place when value systems are seen in a new light, and one workshop objective should be to help each participant experience at least one "aha" moment in which some formerly invisible aspect of culture suddenly becomes obvious. Sometimes it is helpful for facilitators to share their own past "aha" moments.

Creating Emotional Safety

No matter what its focus, professional development, like education in general, is most effective when participants feel emotionally safe. This is especially true when professional development touches on beliefs that can feel very personal, in this instance, beliefs about childrearing and how people relate to each other and the world. Participants may feel vulnerable when sharing personal, culture-based beliefs and experiences related to these topics, particularly if their own value system differs from that of the dominant culture. And whether their beliefs are mainstream or not, people may well feel defensive when their ways of looking at the world are questioned. Thus, it is important to establish trust at the beginning of any presentation so that all can have a more comfortable and productive experience.

Trust building begins with the facilitator. "The clearer the structure and the more secure you are in the role of facilitator, the better the chances for a safe climate and productive discussion" (Mesa-Bains & Shulman, 1994, p. 6). Facilitators who understand the complexity of how cultural values relate to human behavior may be more attuned to participants' nonverbal cues and may be more comfortable reframing questions than those who are unsure. Also, learning more about each other is, itself, trust building. One way to help seed trust within the group is to build informal interaction time into the training; facilitators often find that they learn more about participants and participants learn more about each other during break-time conversations when people do not feel "officially" engaged in formal dialogue.

Upfront "safety" rules or participation guidelines can be developed collaboratively with the group or proposed by the facilitator and adapted by the group. Although some groups function fine without such rules, we have often found them useful in presentations on culture and other diversity-related topics. There need not be many. Establishing a code of confidentiality where information shared within the workshop is considered private and not to be repeated outside the workshop may be particularly important so that participants feel less vulnerable when discussing personal beliefs or experiences. Another rule worth considering is one requiring respectful, nonjudgmental listening to one speaker at a time. However, keep in mind that while listening quietly is a sign of interest in some cultures, in other cultures interruptions are considered a sign of interest and involvement. Therefore, it is important to be alert for different ways that audiences participate and show interest.

Discussions about cultural values can engender strong emotional reactions. While talking about cultural differences, some participants may become aware that they have abandoned their own cultural roots to be successful in the mainstream culture—a realization that can be emotionally wrenching. Some participants may believe that their values are "better" than another person's values, which can cause tension within a group. Both situations require sensitive handling. When a participant expresses a sense of cultural loss, facilitators should acknowledge it because there is a psychic cost to adapting to the dominant culture (Wong Fillmore, 1996). If it seems that some participants are inclined to declare certain values superior or inferior, the facilitator needs to remind the group that in learning about culture one needs to suspend judgment, but that doing so does not require giving up one's own values. Conflicts between cultural values should be identified as a shared problem that needs to be resolved by both parties (Girard & Koch, 1996).

Making Room for Different Ways of Learning

Facilitators need to tailor activity formats to suit participants' learning and participation styles. Some people learn by listening, others need to speak about what they are experiencing, and still others like to write down their ideas and think them over. To the degree possible, the workshop experience should accommodate all ways of learning.

Similarly, facilitators should try to accommodate participants' personal styles. For example, in a large group, some people will be eager to share personal stories while others will be more reticent. Assuming there is adequate time, it makes sense to conduct at least some activities in small groups, or even with pairs, to allow all participants to share their thoughts and feelings without engaging the entire audience.

At the beginning and end of the module, there are opportunities for participants to write, but not all participants will be comfortable writing, especially in a constrained period. Some may use English as a second language and be proficient in writing in their home language only. Others may simply not be comfortable sharing their writing. The facilitator needs to offer alternatives, such as talking to a partner or small group discussion so that no one is left out or feels uncomfortable.

Presentation Tips

Most of the following strategies for preparing to present new material are self-evident, but they may be useful to some new presenters:

- Practice new material in advance, out loud, to see if there are new concepts or terms that could trip you up.

- Mark up the margins of this module with your own notes or references.
- Use a highlighter on points you don't want to forget.
- When possible, practice in front of a friendly audience to gather constructive comments before the actual presentation.

Preparing the Materials

You may wish to detach or photocopy the script and notes, handouts, and overhead transparencies. The handouts and overhead transparencies are in a format that can be easily duplicated. (These materials are copyrighted; therefore, the copyright and citation *must* remain on the copies.) The module is three-hole punched so that you may easily store it in a binder to which you can add materials, such as the *Bridging Cultures Readings* and other resources that complement the module.

Handouts

Handouts are important. Be sure you have copied enough handouts for all participants. In our own presentations, we have usually copied different materials in a variety of colors to make them easy to find and identify during the workshop. Many participants like to have written information to refer to or to share with colleagues.

Agenda

Make an agenda that specifically outlines what you plan to do (see sample in Appendix A). Participants like to know where they are going in a workshop (and they usually like to know when a break is coming too!). Develop an evaluation. You can use the one included in Appendix B (Handout 6) or develop your own. Bring blank overhead transparency sheets and marking pens for taking notes. Recording what people say is both helpful for and respectful of participants. By documenting participants' responses, you will also have a written record that may be useful later in evaluating their understanding of the content and helping you improve your next training.

Checking the Room and Equipment

The room should be large enough to allow comfortable seating for all participants. Ideally, they should sit facing the facilitator so they can easily view the projected overheads. Participants will also need a place to write; having them sit at a desk or table is helpful. If participants are to work sometimes in pairs or small groups, there must be enough room for them to move easily around the room.

Make sure the overhead projector is in good working order and additional light bulbs are available if needed. If the room is very large, you may need a microphone and speakers. Be careful about cords and other obstacles that can affect how you position yourself. Many of these points seem like common sense, but if they are not anticipated, problems with space and equipment can undermine an otherwise effective presentation.

Appendix E

Pilot-Testing Results for the BC–ECE Training Module 2-Hour Workshop

To gather formative feedback for development of the Bridging Cultures in Early Care and Education workshop, the authors pilot tested it sequentially in four venues: the annual leadership institute of the NAEYC; an in-service institute on working with special needs populations produced by the Head Start Division of the Los Angeles County Office of Education (LACOE); a graduate course in early childhood education at California State University, Northridge; and an in-service training for educational specialists, also produced by the LACOE's Head Start division.

Evaluation forms were distributed at each presentation. In addition to asking participants to rate the workshop overall, using a scale of 1 (*not informative*) to 5 (*very informative*), the form asked open-ended questions about various aspects of the workshop. The workshop script and supporting materials presented in this book were revised based on some of the feedback. Thus, because the four workshops took place sequentially, each of the last three was slightly different from the prior workshops.

Overall, participants across the four venues reported finding the workshop information valuable for their professional practice. The average per-session rating ranged from 4.15 at the NAEYC conference (at which the 45 respondents included college and community college instructors, directors or supervisors in various early childhood programs, curriculum developers, and preschool and elementary school teachers) to 4.52 at the final LACOE Head Start presentation (at which most of the 45 participants were child development supervisors). Across the board, participants identified as most meaningful and useful the workshop information—and examples—about differences between those who have a collectivistic perspective and those who have a more individualistic perspective.

Participants in the first pilot test, at the NAEYC Leadership Institute, also noted the value of making people more *conscious* of cultural issues, as one put it, of "making cultural connections visible and proactively part of the conversation." Another expressed appreciation for presenters' willingness to "struggle with us—acknowledging that this is a complex topic, presenting a framework to help think about issues, rather than give solutions." Yet another noted the framework's usefulness as a "tool for understanding often confusing behavior."

Suggested Improvements. One Japanese American participant suggested that in contrasting the "U.S. culture" to "immigrant culture," the workshop misses cultural issues faced by the children and grandchildren of immigrants, who also have had to struggle with integrating both perspectives. Another participant mentioned the desire to understand how the positive aspects of the individualistic perspective might mesh with those of the collectivistic perspective.

To accommodate this feedback, the script was modified to acknowledge that individuals may possess aspects of both the individualistic and collectivistic orientation. The script also stresses the need to view each possible conflict as an opportunity to problem solve and extract a solution that may meet the needs of aspects of both cultural orientations.

The second iteration of the BC–ECE workshop was presented twice at an LACOE in-service training for Head Start staff, once in the morning for 47 people and once in the afternoon for 31. Whereas the afternoon session consisted solely of teachers and teaching assistants, the morning session included a few Head Start program directors and coordinators of special services, such as a disability coordinator and a social services caseworker. Morning participants gave the workshop an average rating of 4.64, and afternoon participants rated at 4.45. When asked about the usefulness of the workshop concepts for their own work, several said it would help them better understand the families with whom they work, why they do certain things, and "how they handle certain situations." One participant wrote of having encountered a number of parents of children with special needs who seemed reluctant to encourage their child's independence, adding, "I think keeping in mind that the families that I serve come from a collectivistic point of view will help [me] serve them efficiently or, at least, understand their parenting styles and try not to judge."

Suggested Improvements. One participant reported finding the workshop information useful but noted that the issues encompassed by the individualism–collectivism framework are "not necessarily this cut and dry." A number of participants asked for more—and more concrete—examples. Others asked for specific strategies that teachers could use in the classroom, as well as more group participation and more discussion time during the workshop.

To address these concerns, the BC–ECE module was modified to include more examples of situations that occur in early childhood settings where individualism and collectivism collide. The module was expanded to include optional activities that allow for more group participation and discussion time. Because the intent of the module is to encourage problem solving when one's own value orientation is in conflict with that of the children and families being served, strategies for classroom use are developed through participants' engagement in several workshop activities. Activity 5, "Thinking about Your Workplace," and Activity 7, "Further Exploration of Patterns," are designed for participants to reflect on conflicts in their own settings and discuss their approaches or resolutions to conflict.

The third iteration of the workshop was presented to 15 graduate students (many of them already working teachers) as part of a course on educational psychology at California State University, Northridge, in the Educational Psychology and Counseling Department. Asked about the most meaningful element of the presentation, students mentioned the value of the examples and of having tangible reasons for people's behavior. One commented that the workshop information "makes you more sensitive to other's cultural values and heightens awareness of different ways to achieve various goals." Another wrote that "cultures are distinct and diverse, and becoming aware of distinctions may be what will resolve so many conflicts that arise in our classroom/school communities." The majority of the students said the BC–ECE information would be helpful with their work with children and families, stressing the connection between behavior and cultural values. One student reported being "more mindful of other cultures, their values and [of] the importance of learning about those values first, before making judgments and recommendations."

Suggested Improvements. Several participants suggested simplifying the vocabulary used in the workshop, adding more visuals, and providing participants with copies of every overhead. All these suggestions were incorporated into the workshop and the materials.

For the final pilot test, the workshop was presented to an audience of 45 LACOE Head Start staff. Rather than being conducted over the standard 2-hour period, the workshop extended over 3 hours. This allowed the presenters to explain the purpose of the session more thoroughly than was possible in the earlier sessions and to devote more time to the evaluation component. Because this represents the culmination of workshop development efforts, more detailed information about participants and their responses is presented here.

The audience was made up largely of child development supervisors but also included education coordinators as well as some resource teachers, area supervisors, transition specialists, and management consultants. Members of many of these role groups are charged with providing professional development to preschool and infant/toddler teachers on a regular basis, and "culture" is one of the topics they need to address. The group was highly diverse in terms of people's ethnicity and cultural backgrounds, which made it ideal for examining the usefulness and meaningfulness of the workshop. Overall, these professionals rated the workshop at 4.52.

As in the prior workshops, this group identified as most meaningful or useful the distinction between individualism and collectivism and the values associated with them. Next in frequency was the importance of raising one's own cultural awareness. In one representative comment, a participant wrote of finding it useful "to identify my own characteristics and why I respond to certain situations the way I do." Another noted that, whether individualistic or collectivistic, people "are entitled to their way of being and dealing with others." One participant said it was valuable to be reminded of how "value systems affect behavior, learning, and relationships." Yet another wrote of coming to understand "how both individualism and collectivism can be a part of one's [own] life."

Participants were also asked what they would like to learn next. The majority wanted more suggestions for applying the information about individualism and collectivism to their own work with parents and staff, for example,

"How to support individualism or collectivism scenarios in a positive way during transitions with child, like home–school–home."

"Strategies for working with families of different cultures."

"About specific problems that agencies have had when there may [have been] a cultural conflict and what specific solutions have been generated."

"More ideas on how we can help staff learn and accept some of the families' culture and traditions."

"I would like to know the impact individualism and collectivism have on cognition."

Participants were also asked whether and how what they learned in the workshop might change the way they work. More than three fourths of them said it would change their practice, and among those who said it would not, most noted that their work or practice already reflected the cultural awareness provided in the workshop. Among those who thought their work would change, many touched generally on how increased awareness about these different ways of viewing the world would inform their thinking about and interaction with staff, parents, and children. Among the wide range of more specific anticipated changes mentioned were reinforcing cultural values on staff evaluations, talking to staff about the importance of listening and observing parents, and talking to staff about how they react to parents and students. Other proposed changes included adding more cultural information during orientation, parent training, and workshops; hiring parents as teacher assistants; surveying and collecting information from throughout the year to be sensitive to families; reviewing potluck policies; and reviewing transition procedures and policies. One respondent noted that although individual policies might not change, "the approach to it can be modified or improved."

Suggested Improvements. Many respondents expressed the wish for more examples, and some suggested having role-playing opportunities in the workshop. Others suggested expanding the presenter group to include teachers and students.

Overall, the workshop feedback indicates that the content and processes of the workshop are effective in engaging participants with the principal BC–ECE concepts and their implications. It also indicates that early childhood professionals want as many concrete examples as possible of the concepts being discussed, would like to see the concepts illustrated or reinforced through multiple media (e.g., handouts, video clips, role playing), and seek opportunities to further personalize application of the content.

With regard to this last point, it is important to recognize that the experiences of individual participants will reflect how culture varies, particularly when it is transplanted to new settings. That said, it is important to help people focus on the notion of "cultural patterns" rather than on the exceptions because individualism and collectivism are connected to patterns in communication, childrearing, and schooling.

The fact that many participants want more time and support is not surprising, but it points to the need for professional developers and teacher educators to consider providing additional time, expanding beyond the basic 2-hour module. Chapter 3 presents suggestions and specific activities for doing so.

Finally, it is likely that any group of participants will be diverse in terms of their relative familiarity with BC–ECE concepts or other relevant knowledge about culture and its impact on childrearing, child care, and education. A successful workshop will draw on the expertise of those who are more knowledgeable and help those who are new to the content feel comfortable enough to explore.

Appendix F

Annotated Bibliography

The following resources provide a conceptual foundation for understanding BC–ECE. Although the list is not exhaustive, the books and articles included address many of the central ideas and perspectives that have given shape to our thinking about cultural differences, parent–child relations, and the individualism–collectivism framework. We hope you find the information relevant and enlightening.

Gallimore, R., Goldenberg, C. N., & Weisner, T. S. (1993). The social construction and subjective reality of activity settings: Implications for community psychology. *American Journal of Community Psychology, 21*, 537–558.

The activities of daily life in which children, families, educators, and caregivers engage are the foundation for much learning and development. Researchers interested in looking at the interrelationships among culturally based values, social context, and daily activities have found the concept of "activity setting" useful. In characterizing an activity setting, they examine the following elements: (a) personnel (people involved in an activity), (b) cultural values and beliefs reflected in the activity, (c) the immediate demands of the task (e.g., those involved in hammering a nail or writing a sentence), (d) the expectations for the ways the activity will be carried out (sometimes called a script), and (e) the purposes or motives of the participants. By combining external descriptors with internal factors such as values and purposes, they believe a more meaningful explanation of the activity can be achieved. For instance, in exploring how parents read a story to their child, it is important to identify their understanding of the task, as well as the values and beliefs they hold related to "reading" or "reading a story."

This article is particularly helpful in developing the reader's understanding of why it is important to push beyond surface descriptions of behaviors. The authors also offer a strong rationale for looking across cultures to find commonalities on which educators and families can build in addressing the needs of children.

Gonzalez-Mena, J. (2005). *Diversity in early care and education: Honoring differences* (4th ed.). New York: McGraw-Hill.

This book is an excellent supplement to *Bridging Cultures in Early Care and Education Module.* Formerly titled *Multicultural Issues in Child Care*, the fourth edition delves deeply into how diversity, equity, and social justice are critical to appropriate early childhood education practice. The book is intended for a broad spectrum of early childhood professionals. It hopes to help them develop an awareness of and sensitivity to cultural differences to reduce cultural conflicts and promote healthy development in children and families. The constructs of individualism and collectivism are discussed in chapter 4 and applied to routines, such as eating and sleeping, commonly found in early childhood and care environments. Other chapters use the individualism–collectivism framework to understand cultural differences in important developmental processes such as attachment, play, and childhood socialization. Using real-life examples from early childhood settings, Gonzalez-Mena illustrates how early childhood professionals can react positively to cultural differences and how they can productively enter into dialogue with parents and others to reach mutually acceptable solutions.

Greenfield, P. M., & Suzuki, L. K. (1998). Culture and human development: Implications for parenting, education, pediatrics, and mental health. In I. E. Sigel & K. A. Renninger (Vol. Eds.), *Handbook of child psychology* (5th ed., pp. 1059–1109). New York: Wiley.

This comprehensive chapter is a superb and readable introduction to the topic of culture and human development. Greenfield and Suzuki show how parents' developmental priorities for their children are influenced by cultural values. They demonstrate how concentrating on "cultural models" rather than discrete behaviors is more productive in understanding the role of culture in childrearing and in the shaping of social institutions such as health care and education. The cultural models of individualism and collectivism are used to explain parental approaches to feeding and sleeping arrangements for their children, expectations for children's behavior, norms of parent–child communication, and attitudes toward attachment. Implications for parents, teachers, and child-care workers as well as pediatricians and other clinicians are discussed.

Note: A revised version of this chapter, with C. Rothstein-Fisch as third author, is to appear in the *Handbook of Child Psychology* (6th ed.) (in press).

Greenfield, P. M., & Cocking, R. R. (Eds.). (1994). *Cross-cultural roots of minority child development.* Hillsdale, NJ: Lawrence Erlbaum Associates.

Researchers from many cultural backgrounds explore how cultural and social histories influence the course of human development. "Minority roots" of child development are emphasized because until recently the field of developmental psychology took a "universal" approach to development based in the norms and values of Western European societies. Once again, the cultural models of individualism and collectivism are invoked to explain essential differences in groups' ways of socializing their children and organizing schooling. The book is divided into sections, with chapters on American (Indigenous), Asian, and African roots; research and personal reports show how interactions between minority and dominant cultures result in adaptation and biculturalism, as well as show the persistence of childrearing values over several generations after immigration or intercultural contact.

Chapters in this book stand on their own so that readers interested in the cultural roots of particular groups can read selectively. The first chapter (by Greenfield) orients the reader to the framework of individualism and collectivism and to the issues addressed in the book.

Kagitcibasi, C. (1996). *Family and human development across cultures: A view from the other side*. Mahwah, NJ: Lawrence Erlbaum Associates.

Using a cross-cultural perspective, Kagitcibasi, a professor of psychology at Koc University in Istanbul, provides an overview of human and family development, recasting individualism as independence and collectivism as interdependence. In her discussion, the idea of the "relational self" is contrasted with the "separated self." The relational self is part of an individual's orientation toward interdependence, and the separated self is part of a person's orientation toward independence.

Chapter 5, entitled "Family and Family Change," is particularly instructive for early childhood professionals dealing with families who possess an interdependent point of reference but must traverse the independent landscape that characterizes early childhood education. In this chapter, Kagitcibasi proposes an emotional interdependence model to help us understand how both the independence and interdependence perspectives can combine in the face of cultural change. In this model, the individual does not need interdependence for material survival but does invest emotionally in relationships at both the individual and family levels. This third approach comes about as individuals and societies move from a more agrarian economic base toward a more modern technologically oriented base. Kagitcibasi discusses how changing societal demands are altering the cultural priorities of many societies. To support her ideas, she provides evidence from the Turkish Early Enrichment Project. Parallel changes are seen in many societies, a topic that is raised in Greenfield and Cocking (1994) as well.

LeVine, R. A. (1988). Human parental care: Universal goals, cultural strategies, individual behavior. In R. A. LeVine, P. M. Miller, & M. M. West (Eds.), *Parental behaviors in diverse societies. New directions for child development, 40*, 3–12. San Francisco: Jossey-Bass.

Robert LeVine, professor of education at Harvard University, has postulated that there exist universal parental goals for children's development. He distinguishes between what parents want *from* their children as being influenced by culture and what parents want *for* their children as being universal. First, parents want survival and health for their children. This is followed by the acquisition of economic capacities (e.g., in the United States this might be reading and math capabilities). Finally, parents want their children to acquire the cultural values of their group or population. These universal parental goals are hierarchical in nature because parents want to be assured of their child's health and survival before they turn their attention to behaviors that would ensure their child's economic security. Similarly, parents give priority to behaviors that would help their child achieve a positive economic future before they stress any particular cultural values.

What is important about these universal parental goals is that they influence forms of parental adaptation to their environment. For example, if parents live in a society where there is high infant mortality, they are likely to organize their behavior around ensuring the health and safety of their infant before they think about issues of intellectual stimulation of the baby. According to LeVine, parents do not blindly follow genetic or cultural rules; rather, parents are rational in their conduct because they adjust their behavior to their perceptions of risk and benefits in their child's environment. Cultural customs are an outgrowth of adaptive practices that have evolved over time.

Ogbu, J. U. (1981). Origins of human competence: A cultural-ecological perspective. *Child Development, 52*, 413–429.

This important essay by John Ogbu was one of the first scholarly efforts to contradict the deficit model that was broadly applied to ethnic and racial minority children and families in the late 1960s. Ogbu argues that human competence should be defined within an individual's cultural context and that one should not view one cultural context as being better or superior to another but rather should try to understand minority childrearing and development on its own terms. According to Ogbu, childrearing patterns are influenced by instrumental competencies needed to function successfully as an adult in the societal context in which an individual resides. Offering a cultural-ecological model to understanding human competence, Ogbu views the environment in which an individual develops as one where the level of technology and knowledge and the nature of available resources influence the tasks and behaviors necessary to succeed in that environment. This model assumes that every culture maintains, albeit largely unconsciously, an image of what it means to be a successful adult. This image, in turn, guides its childrearing practices, which aim to engender in children the personal characteristics needed for success in that culture.

The cultural-ecological model provides a rationale for understanding parental values, beliefs, and behaviors, and how parents' cultural backgrounds influence the way they think about child growth and development. Understanding that the skills and competencies valued by any group is tied to the demands of the environment in which they were reared helps early childhood professionals view cultural differences as having a rational and sound basis.

Rogoff, B. (2003). *The cultural nature of human development.* Oxford, England: Oxford University Press.

Rogoff, a professor of psychology who has conducted research in a Mayan community in Guatemala for three decades, has written an engaging book filled with photographs of families from many cultural backgrounds. Wary of generalizations, Rogoff nevertheless effectively shows how the examination of patterns in communities' childrearing practices can be useful to understanding important differences and similarities between cultures. She notes in her first chapter, "People develop as participants in cultural communities. Their development can be understood only in light of the cultural practices and circumstances of their communities—which also change" (p. 4). Rogoff deals with families within the contexts of their communities, exploring issues such as gender and age expectations, roles of children, adolescence as a special stage, and initiation into adulthood. She shows how context interacts with cognitive development and how notions of intelligence vary from culture to culture. The final section of the book addresses cultural continuity and change across time, with an emphasis on the dynamic nature of culture.

Schieffelin, B. B., & Ochs, E. (Eds.). (1986). *Language socialization across cultures.* Cambridge, MA: Cambridge University Press.

This edited volume explores the connections between language development and culture. Several studies are presented that show how culture socializes children through language and how children are socialized to use language in culturally specific ways. For example, in some cultures children are treated as adults during conversations, and in other cultures children are expected to be observers with information communicated through shared activities. An important conclusion that can be drawn from these studies is that as children learn language, they develop a foundation of shared meaning with their group which, in turn, colors their view of the world.

Super, C. M., & Harkness, S. (1986). The developmental niche: A conceptualization at the interface of child and culture. *International Journal of Behavioral Development, 9*, 545–569.

Super and Harkness introduce the concept of the "developmental niche" as a means of understanding the role of culture in development. The developmental niche consists of a child's physical and social setting, the customs and practices of child care and childrearing, and the psychology of the caregivers, especially what the authors call "parental ethnotheories." Consistencies in these aspects of the developmental niche provide information to developing children about their culture's expectations for them. One of the important correlates of the developmental niche construct for early childhood professionals is that parental ethnotheories, or belief systems, are derived from their individual cultural backgrounds. These parental beliefs set the stage for understanding a developing child's capabilities and knowing how best to interact with children to achieve a particular developmental goal.

References

BANDTEC: A Network for Diversity Training. (2003, April). *Reaching for answers: A workbook on diversity in early childhood education*. Oakland, CA: BANDTEC.

Barks, C., Nicholson, R., Arberry, A. J., & Moyne, J. (2004). *The essential Rumi*. San Francisco: Harper.

Barrera, I., with Corso, R. M., & Macpherson, D. (2003). *Skilled dialogue: Strategies for responding to cultural diversity in early childhood*. Baltimore: Brookes.

Bowman, B. T., & Stott, F. M. (1994). Understanding development in a cultural context: The challenge for teachers. In B. L. Mallory & R. S. New (Eds.), *Diversity and developmentally appropriate practices: Challenges for early childhood education*. New York: Teachers College Press.

Bredekamp, S., & Copple, C. (Eds.). (1997). *Developmentally appropriate practice in early childhood programs* (Rev. ed.). Washington, DC: National Association for the Education of Young Children.

Child Trends. (1997). *Number of children under age 18 in the United States*. Retrieved October 28, 2003, from http://www.childtrendsdatabank.org/indicators/53NumberofChildren.cfm

Cushner, K., & Brislin, R. W. (1995). *Intercultural interactions: A practical guide*. Thousand Oaks, CA: Sage.

Delgado-Gaitan, C. (1994). Socializing young children in Mexican-American families: An intergenerational perspective. In P. M. Greenfield & R. R. Cocking (Eds.), *Cross-cultural roots of minority child development* (pp. 55–86). Hillsdale, NJ: Lawrence Erlbaum Associates.

Derman-Sparks, L., & the Antibias Curriculum Task Force. (1989). *Antibias curriculum: Tools for empowering young children*. Washington, DC: National Association for the Education of Young Children.

Derman-Sparks, L., & Phillips, C. B. (1997). *Teaching/learning anti-racism: A developmental approach*. New York: Teachers College Press.

Friend, M., & Cook, L. (2003). *Interactions: Collaboration skills for school professionals* (4th ed.). Boston: Allyn & Bacon.

Girard, K., & Koch, S. J. (1996). *Conflict resolution in the schools: A manual for educators.* San Francisco: Jossey-Bass.

Goldenberg, C. N., Gallimore, R., Reese, L. J., & Garnier, H. (2001). Cause or effect? A longitudinal study of immigrant Latino parents' aspirations and expectations and their children's school performance. *American Educational Research Journal, 38*, 547–582.

Gonzalez-Mena, J. (2001). *Multicultural issues in child care.* New York: WCB/McGraw-Hill.

Greenfield, P. M. (1994). Independence and interdependence as developmental scripts: Implications for theory, research, and practice. In P. M. Greenfield & R. R. Cocking (Eds.), *Cross-cultural roots of minority child development* (pp. 1–37). Hillsdale, NJ: Lawrence Erlbaum Associates.

Greenfield, P. M., & Cocking, R. R. (Eds.). (1994). *Cross-cultural roots of minority child development.* Hillsdale, NJ: Lawrence Erlbaum Associates.

Greenfield, P. M., Quiroz, B., & Raeff, C. (2000). Cross-cultural conflict and harmony in the social construction of the child. In S. Harkness, C. Raeff, & C. M. Super (Eds.), *Variability in the social construction of the child: New directions for child and adolescent development, 87*, 93–108. San Francisco: Jossey-Bass.

Greenfield, P. M., & Suzuki, L. K. (1998). Culture and human development: Implications for parenting, education, pediatrics, and mental health. In I. E. Sigel & K. A. Renninger (Eds.), *Handbook of child psychology: Vol. 4. Child psychology in practice* (pp. 1059–1109). New York: Wiley.

Guerra, P., & Garcia, S. B. (2000). *Understanding the cultural contexts of teaching and learning.* Austin, TX: Southwest Educational Development Laboratory.

Harwood, R. L., Miller, J. G., & Irizzary, N. L. (1995). *Culture and attachment: Perceptions of the child in context.* New York: Guilford.

Head Start. (1992). *Multicultural principles for Head Start Programs.* Available at www.bmcc.org/Headstart/Cultural/

Henderson, A. T., & Mapp, K. L. (2002). *A new wave of evidence: The impact of school, family, and community connections on student achievement.* Austin, TX: National Center for Family & Community Connections with Schools, Southwest Educational Development Laboratory.

Hofstede, G. (2001). *Culture's consequences: Comparing values, behaviors, institutions, and organizations across nations* (2nd ed.). Thousand Oaks, CA: Sage.

Hyson, M. (Ed.). (2003). *Preparing early childhood professionals: NAEYC's standards for programs.* Washington, DC: National Association for the Education of Young Children.

Lally, J. R. (1995). The impact of child care policies and practices on infant/toddler formation. *Young Children, 51*, 58–67.

Lindsey, R. B., Nuri Robins, K., & Terrell, R. D. (2003). *Cultural proficiency: A manual for school leaders* (2nd ed.). Thousand Oaks, CA: Corwin.

Lustig, M. W., & Koester, J. (2003). *Intercultural competence: Interpersonal communication across cultures* (4th ed.). New York: Addison Wesley Longman.

Lynch, E. W., & Hanson, M. J. (1998). *Developing cross-cultural competence: A guide for working with children and their families* (2nd ed.). Baltimore: Brookes.

Mesa-Bains, A., & Shulman, J. H. (1994). *Diversity in the classroom: Facilitator's guide*. Hillsdale, NJ: Lawrence Erlbaum Associates.

McKinnon, J. (2003). The Black population in the United States: March 2002. *Current population reports* (pp. 20–541). Washington, DC: U.S. Census Bureau.

Moll, L. C., Amanti, C., Neff, D., & Gonzalez, N. (1992). Funds of knowledge for teaching: Using a qualitative approach to connect homes and classrooms. *Theory Into Practice, 31*, 132–141.

Morelli, G. A., Rogoff, B., Oppenheim, D., & Goldsmith, D. (1992). Cultural variations in infants' sleep arrangements: Questions of independence. *Developmental Psychology, 28*, 604–613.

Ogunwole, S. U. (2003). The American Indian and Alaska Native population: 2000. *Census 2000 Brief* (C2KBR/01-15). Washington, DC: U.S. Census Bureau.

Patterson, K., Grenny, J., McMillan, R., & Switzler, A. (2002). *Crucial conversations: Tools for talking when the stakes are high*. New York: McGraw-Hill.

Program for Infant/Toddler Caregivers. (1995). *Trainer's manual, module IV: Culture, family, and providers* (S. Signer, Ed.). San Francisco: WestEd.

Raeff, C., Greenfield, P. M., & Quiroz, B. (2000). Conceptualizing interpersonal relationships in cultural contexts of individualism and collectivism. In S. Harkness, C. Raeff, & C. M. Super (Eds.), *Variability in the social construction of the child: New directions for child and adolescent development, 87*, 59–74. San Francisco: Jossey-Bass.

Ramirez, R. R., & de la Cruz, G. P. (2003). The Hispanic population in the United States: March 2002. *Current population reports* (pp. 20–545). Washington, DC: U.S. Census Bureau.

Reese, L. (2002). Parental strategies in contrasting cultural settings: Families in Mexico and "El Norte." *Anthropology & Education Quarterly, 33*, 30–59.

Reeves, T., & Bennett, C. (2003). The Asian and Pacific Islander population in the United States: March 2002. *Current population reports* (pp. 20–540). Washington, DC: U.S. Census Bureau.

Rogoff, B. (2003). *The cultural nature of human development*. New York: Oxford University Press.

Rothstein-Fisch, C. (2003a). *Bridging cultures: Teacher education module*. Mahwah, NJ: Lawrence Erlbaum Associates.

Rothstein-Fisch, C. (2003b). *Readings for bridging cultures: Teacher education module*. Mahwah, NJ: Lawrence Erlbaum Associates.

Rothstein-Fisch, C., Greenfield, P. M., & Trumbull, E. (1999). Bridging cultures with classroom strategies. *Educational Leadership, 56*(7), 64–67.

Shonkoff, J. P., & Phillips, D. A. (2000). *From neurons to neighborhoods: The science of early childhood development*. Washington, DC: National Academy Press.

Shweder, R. A., Goodnow, J., Hatano, G., LeVine, R. A., Markus, H., & Miller, P. (1998). The cultural psychology of development: One mind, many mentalities. In W. Damon & R. M. Lerner (Eds.), *Handbook of child psychology: Vol. 1. Theoretical models of human development* (5th ed., pp. 865–937). New York: Wiley.

Triandis, H. C. (1989). Cross-cultural studies of individualism and collectivism. *Nebraska Symposium on Motivation, 37*, 43–133.

Trumbull, E., Diaz-Meza, R., Hasan, A., & Rothstein-Fisch, C. (2001). *Five-year report of the Bridging Cultures Project: 1996–2000*. San Francisco: WestEd. Available at http://www.WestEd.org/BridgingCultures

Trumbull, E., & Farr, B. (2005). *Language and learning: What teachers need to know*. Norwood, MA: Christopher-Gordon.

Trumbull, E., Greenfield, P. M., & Quiroz, B. (2004). Cultural values in learning and education. In B. Williams (Ed.), *Closing the achievement gap* (2nd ed., pp. 67–98). Alexandria, VA: ASCD.

Trumbull, E., Greenfield, P., Rothstein-Fisch, C., & Maynard, A. (2005). From altered perceptions to altered practice: Teachers bridge cultures in the classroom. In P. M. Greenfield, A. Isaac, E. Trumbull, C. Rothstein-Fisch, & B. Quiroz (Eds.), *Bridging cultures in Latino immigrant education*. Manuscript in preparation.

Trumbull, E., Greenfield, P. M., Rothstein-Fisch, C., & Quiroz, B. (2001). *Bridging cultures between home and school: A guide for teachers*. Mahwah, NJ: Lawrence Erlbaum Associates.

Trumbull, E., Rothstein-Fisch, C., & Hernandez, E. (2003). Parent involvement—According to whose values? *School Community Journal, 13*(2), 45–72.

Varner, I., & Beamer, L. (2004). *Intercultural communication in the global workplace* (3rd ed.). Boston: McGraw-Hill/Irwin.

Wong Fillmore, L. (1996). What happens when languages are lost? An essay on language assimilation and cultural identity. In D. I. Slobin & J. Gerhardt (Eds.), *Social interaction, social context and language: Essays in honor of Susan Ervin-Tripp* (pp. 655–670). Mahwah, NJ: Lawrence Erlbaum Associates.

Author Index

G

H

I

K

L

M

N

O

P

For Product Safety Concerns and Information please contact our EU
representative GPSR@taylorandfrancis.com Taylor & Francis Verlag GmbH,
Kaufingerstraße 24, 80331 München, Germany

Printed and bound by CPI Group (UK) Ltd, Croydon, CR0 4YY
20/06/2025
01904321-0001